"The single most powerful tool I've encountered to gain emotional intelligence is the Enneagram. It's given me a level of self-awareness that almost feels like magical insight. If you want to better yourself, read Scott's book. Beware, though—before he wrote it he may have read your diary."

Donald Miller, author, speaker, and CEO of
StoryBrand and Business Made Simple

"In *The Enneagram of Emotional Intelligence* Scott Allender has provided a practical, accessible, and yet profound guide to living a better life through self-understanding grounded in a clearly articulated and effective integration of EQ and the Enneagram and in his own personal experience of transformation."

Beatrice Chestnut, PhD, author of *The Complete Enneagram*,
The 9 Types of Leadership, and coauthor of
The Enneagram Guide to Waking Up

"*The Enneagram of Emotional Intelligence* offers an incisive perspective on why it doesn't work to white-knuckle sustainable, soul-level change—and what to do instead. Using insights from the Enneagram, emotional intelligence coaching, and decades of experience in leadership, Allender guides readers to understand and apply their Enneagram knowledge for personal and professional development. I've read dozens of Enneagram books, but this is one that will stick with me, and I anticipate recommending it time and again."

Stephanie Barron Hall, author, Enneagram practitioner,
and creator of @NineTypesCo

"In *The Enneagram of Emotional Intelligence*, Scott Allender brings together a powerful set of insights and tools to help us hold on to our humanity in every aspect of our work and lives. Wisdom

T0051236

and warmth pervade every page in this compelling blueprint for greater self-awareness."

Jean Gomes, author of *Leading in a Non-Linear World*
and *The Way We're Working Isn't Working*

"*The Enneagram of Emotional Intelligence* is the guidebook you've been waiting for. Scott Allender uses the insight of the Enneagram to make the concept of emotional intelligence practical, authentic, and engaging. Readers will leave with both greater self-awareness and greater understanding for the people they interact with every day."

Jeremy Cowart, artist and author of *I'm Possible*

THE
ENNEAGRAM
of EMOTIONAL
INTELLIGENCE

A Journey to Personal and Professional Success

SCOTT ALLENDER

BakerBooks
a division of Baker Publishing Group
Grand Rapids, Michigan

Published by Baker Books
a division of Baker Publishing Group
PO Box 6287, Grand Rapids, MI 49516-6287
www.bakerbooks.com

Printed in the United States of America

Library of Congress Cataloging-in-Publication Data
Names: Allender, Scott, author.
Title: The Enneagram of emotional intelligence : a journey to personal and professional success / Scott Allender.
Description: Grand Rapids, MI : Baker Books, a division of Baker Publishing Group, [2023] | Includes bibliographical references.
Identifiers: LCCN 2022035882 | ISBN 9781540902764 (paperback) | ISBN 9781540902979 (casebound) | ISBN 9781493439614 (ebook)
Subjects: LCSH: Enneagram. | Emotional intelligence. | Mindfulness (Psychology) | Transformative learning.
Classification: LCC BF698.35.E54 A45 2023 | DDC 155.2/6—dc23/eng/20221014
LC record available at https://lccn.loc.gov/2022035882

Some names and details have been changed to protect the privacy of the individuals involved.

Published in association with The Bindery Agency, www.TheBinderyAgency.com.

Baker Publishing Group publications use paper produced from sustainable forestry practices and post-consumer waste whenever possible.

23   24   25   26   27   28   29   7   6   5   4   3   2   1

For Kristin, Kenzie, and Selah

What lies behind you and what lies in front of you,
pales in comparison to what lies inside of you.
—Ralph Waldo Emerson

CONTENTS

FOREWORD

These days, a simple online search about emotional intelligence or the Enneagram will give a host of easily digestible guides and engaging charts. You can find anything—from what movie character fits your personality to the best breakfast food according to your birth date. But there's a massive difference between collecting information and doing the deep, good work of personal transformation. This book in your hand is about transformation—the kind that starts deep within then ripples outward into every area of your life.

It's telling that no matter how much we learn about our personality traits, quirks, and tendencies, we're still hungry to learn more. And from years of teaching and counseling, I know this hunger is drawn from a truth we feel but often don't allow ourselves to fully realize: there's more within us that we don't understand than that which we do. There is much more to be discovered beneath our conscious awareness.

My friend Scott Allender peels back the cloudy veil that prevents us from accessing holistic self-awareness at three levels.

First, he will guide you to emotional intelligence through the only sustainable pathway possible: emotional healing. As Scott so expertly explains, we need to heal the way we experience and interpret emotions in order to become emotionally adept.

Second, Scott will help you unearth the self-limiting beliefs you hold about yourself. You can't receive new programming if the old, outdated system is still running the script.

Third, by the time you close this book, you'll have made peace with yourself. You'll be given a guide for integrating all of your wonderful traits with the parts of yourself you've been denying. This is ridiculously good news. Your energy will be used less on fighting the obstacles between who you are and who you want to be and more on moving effectively and successfully in the world as a more emotionally whole person. The hunger to unlock your own inner workings will be satisfied, and you'll be free to set out on the life of wholeness.

When Scott told me he was working on this book, I wasn't surprised. It made perfect sense for Scott to guide you, the reader, on the journey ahead because he's been where you are and is walking the difficult path of personal growth. The journey to real, lasting transformation involves hard work, but I can attest that it will be the most important work you'll ever do.

Ian Morgan Cron, author of *The Story of You: An Enneagram Journey to Becoming Your True Self*

ACKNOWLEDGMENTS

I wrote this book standing on the shoulders of Enneagram giants. While too numerous to list them all (lest I risk unintentionally omitting any key contributors to the advancement of Enneagram study), there have been a few particularly powerful voices in my journey so far, including but not limited to Claudio Naranjo, Helen Palmer, David Daniels, Don Richard Riso, Sandra Maitri, and my personal teachers, mentors, and friends, Beatrice Chestnut, Uranio Paes, and Ian Morgan Cron.

Without their work, this book wouldn't be possible. Their wisdom has changed the lives of countless students and set me on a path of self-discovery that I wouldn't have found without them. It is my sincere hope that, in some small way, this book makes a positive contribution to the conversation. As you read, hold everything I say lightly, but please don't reject any of it at face value either. Sit with it, consider it, test it, and see what comes up for you. If the content in this book helps you to do that, then I'll consider it a success.

INTRODUCTION

Something Isn't Right

I saw the angel in the marble and carved until I set him free.

Michelangelo

I pulled onto the exit ramp and prayed that I wouldn't faint while driving my car. My heart pounded erratically, and I felt light-headed and tingly all over as I struggled to breathe. Having never experienced anything like this, I concluded that I was dying.

I was in an unfamiliar town and fearing for my life, so I pulled over and dialed 911. I don't really remember what I said on the phone, but the dispatcher responded that paramedics were on their way. I got out of the car and started pacing. Soon I heard sirens in the distance, and moments later, I saw the ambulance. Then, just as the ambulance approached me, I found my breath again and my heart settled into a normal, quieter rhythm. I began to feel okay . . . *and quite foolish*.

The paramedics gave me an EKG and I "passed." However, I recalled that my mother-in-law had once passed an EKG during an *actual* heart attack, so I wasn't all that reassured. The paramedics told me I should come to the hospital for more tests just to be safe, but I was nearly two thousand miles from home, so I did what I thought was the most sensible thing.

I declined.

I found out later that I'd experienced an anxiety attack. But even as the paramedics drove away that day, I felt as if I had just scratched the surface of a very deep issue. Later that day, I asked myself for the very first time: *What am I really feeling? And why don't I already know?*

Those simple questions helped me realize something I had ignored for most of my life: I didn't know what I was feeling because I didn't grow up with the sense that my feelings mattered. My early childhood home was unpredictable. My parents were well-intentioned and loving people individually, but when they were together, it was a combustible combination.

Walking into a room they occupied required finely tuned discernment to quickly determine if the room was on the verge of becoming toxic. While any other onlookers usually remained clueless to impending threats, I quickly became a skilled navigator, learning to divert toxicity for both myself and others.

I learned to read a room and people with sometimes astonishing precision. And more importantly, I learned to look for and identify the redemptive edge in most challenges. Much later in life, these experiences allowed me to help other people navigate their own stories and solve some of their greatest personal and organizational challenges. In fact, helping others find growth and wholeness from the inside out is my primary motivation for writing this book.

Mastering the skill of reading a room taught me when it was time to leave or when I needed to shift my expectations because we weren't going to that family movie after all or because the family excursion to Disneyland was about to go south.

But those skills came with a cost. I felt wanted when I was the family relationship broker, and I became the one everyone in my family leaned on. After my parents divorced, I adapted to the expectations of the parent whose house I was visiting. Who I was on a Monday with Mom was vastly different from who I was on a Friday night with Dad, and I learned that my own feelings and identity didn't have a place in the narrative. I also began to believe that people don't value others for who they are but for what they do.

None of this happened on a conscious level, but it became an essential strategy for my survival. And when my needs weren't met, I would double down on this strategy, becoming even *more* of what other people wanted from me. Most of the time it worked. I grew up, started a career, began a family, and climbed the ladder of success. The more I succeeded, the further I was drifting from my truest self. But I received accolades and just enough admiration to keep me believing that I was doing fine. Thriving, even. I confused *seeming* with *being* and just kept going. Until that fateful moment when I found myself unable to breathe on the highway.

From the moment I veered toward the exit at seventy miles per hour, my coping strategies took a sharp turn. I soon began to realize that the tactics and narratives I'd learned in childhood—that my feelings and personal identity were unimportant, that it's what you achieve that matters, that you should never let them see you sweat—were lies.

Instead of being the place where I breathed my last, that parking lot was where I finally started to wake up.

Inside Monstro the Whale

I once heard Enneagram teacher and author Ian Cron explain that his favorite spiritual book was, surprisingly, *Pinocchio*. "He's a boy who was born yet is not real," Cron explained. "And though he's merely animated, he longs to be real." In the story, Pinocchio sets off on a journey to become real, but along the way he has several misadventures. He joins a circus in hopes of becoming a star, yet he ends up in jail. After his release, he continues sowing his wild oats, going to Pleasure Island where he smokes, plays pool, drinks, and even throws a brick through a church window. None of it makes him feel real, however. Disappointed, he returns home to his father, Geppetto, but doesn't find him. Geppetto has already left in search of his son, so Pinocchio heads out after him. This search leads Pinocchio into the literal belly of the beast: he has to let himself be swallowed by Monstro the whale in order to rescue Geppetto. Cron sees this as a metaphor for spiritual transformation: "In the process of going into the dark shadow of the whale, he drowns and dies. Only then is he resurrected by the Blue Fairy. As he awakens, he's relieved to discover he has become a real boy. He has traversed the sacred journey from the false self to the true self."

Over the years since that life-shifting anxiety attack, I've done extensive internal work to move closer to my truest self. I've been certified in various psychometric tools, gone on retreats, engaged in coaching, and spent a good deal of time in therapy. However, nothing has been more effective for me personally and professionally than working with the Enneagram to journey away from falseness—from the fragility of ego to a stronger and more authentic self. The Enneagram has been my vehicle for releasing my false narratives and stepping into a truer story: the story of who I was before my childhood experiences told me who I needed to become in order to gain approval and belonging. This growth work has enabled me to become a more centered, integrated, and effective person, husband, father, leader, and friend. My successes now are richer and more meaningful because my work is rooted in a place of greater personal value, sincerity, and purpose. I pay less attention to success and more attention to my heart. And I know a similar journey is possible for you.

Regardless of where you are at this moment, I believe that somewhere in each of us is a sense that something's not quite right. There's a distance between who we want to be and where we find ourselves. We feel disconnected from the truest, best versions of ourselves. We get stuck in stories about who we are that may have been useful to us once but are no longer true (and perhaps never were). Even worse, these stories and the unconscious motivations that keep them alive often produce the exact opposite of the outcomes we desire. We want loving relationships, but our behavior drives others away; we want career success, but we keep unconsciously sabotaging our own efforts at work. We are our own self-fulfilling prophecies. This happened with my parents who, I believe, were sincere each and every time they professed their love to one another. But then something would happen, triggering a hurt-filled and toxic reaction to each other. They were unable to truly see themselves. Each judged the other by their actions while judging themselves by their intentions until it was all irredeemable.

The core beliefs and attitudes we carry get us stuck in reactive patterns to all of life's stimuli and stressors. We have triggers and people who trigger us. We let certain things (and certain someones) get the best of us. We yell at traffic, snap at the kids, and forget to say thank you to our best team members. We often struggle to believe in ourselves. Maybe we feel underappreciated and are always coveting more praise, recognition, and reward. Or maybe we don't know *what* we feel, and we hide from the probing it would take to find out by looking for a new job or an exciting experience every twelve to eighteen months. We may feel restlessness most of the time. Or maybe we get that big promotion we've been chasing and feel . . . nothing.

These are all products of the denied self—and they become patterns and behaviors that keep us from being fully present. They prevent us from completely accepting ourselves and others and block us from vulnerability and relational intimacy. Because of these patterns, we are unable to create and sustain the organizational cultures, families, and relationships we say we want.

You may be nowhere near an anxiety attack like the one I experienced, but the following are signs that may indicate your true self is being denied:

- You feel sad much of the time.
- You experience unexplained anger or subtle irritation almost every day, and you cannot seem to figure out why or what to do about it.
- You have the impulse to be busy, always doing something, and can never seem to quiet your mind.
- You are chronically concerned with what others think about you. Are you liked, loved, wanted?
- You regularly experience exhaustion and weariness without an obvious cause.
- Most days you appear fine to others, but you often feel like you're on the outside looking in at a world in which you don't quite fit.
- You sense that you could be a healthier leader, partner, team member, or friend.

Wherever you find yourself today, thriving in this life is predicated upon awareness. We cannot know true intimacy, friendship, or joy if we don't know ourselves. We cannot be close to another if we are far from ourselves. And we cannot develop and sustain a healthy emotional climate until we surface and unlock the hidden patterns and behaviors that keep us blocked from the emotional wisdom we covet and that our world so desperately needs.

To free ourselves from the hidden forces that are holding us back is the goal of this book. I invite you to journey with me as we dive deeper into the world of emotional intelligence and its impact on our lives. As an emotional intelligence coach, I often see how we can have all the data we need from a self-reported assessment, a 360 feedback report, or professional coaching sessions yet be unable to link the data to any real change in ourselves. We may already *know* that EQ is more important than IQ when it comes to success or failure. However, very few people are able to achieve and maintain a healthy EQ, even though it can be developed!

Why? What is blocking us from becoming more emotionally intelligent in a meaningful and sustainable way?

What if emotional intelligence isn't about dialing up one desirable attribute while turning down a lesser one? What if true emotional intelligence requires a metamorphosis that mere information plus willpower cannot give us? What if, to emerge as emotionally literate, wise, and holistically intelligent beings, we first need to enter Monstro the whale?

How Do We Get There?

As we begin this journey inward, we have to acknowledge the ways in which we've gotten stuck. The chapters that follow will discuss various ways that our dominant Enneagram type's vice has been showing up in us—how it's locked us in repetitive patterns of predictable, automated behaviors. These keep us lulled into a zombie-like sleep state, meandering from one thing to another, barely awake to the experience of our own lives, especially when we are running around like mad trying to get through our eternal to-do lists.

I'm setting you on a never-ending path of self-discovery. *Never-ending?!* Well, yes. But it's not as daunting as it might sound at first. The truth is, there is no "self-awareness station" where we'll finally arrive if we can just figure out which trains to board. The moment you think you've finally mastered your self-awareness is the very moment your self-awareness begins to deteriorate. As our world evolves and life unfolds, our call to action is to stay on the growth path, continually reflecting, observing, and learning. We must learn to keep coming back to ourselves when faced with life's general stressors, complex relationship dynamics, painful decisions, and wins and losses.

We'll start with a guide to the basics of the Enneagram (the nine personality types, their basic motivations, and their typical behaviors) before delving into what emotional intelligence is and why it's so important (part 1). Then we'll explore five different emotional intelligence measures (from self-perception to stress management) and learn what our Enneagram type might look like when we are in low awareness and high awareness (part 2). We'll finish the book by learning about some core practices that can keep us living honestly and authentically (part 3).

When I talk about different levels of awareness, they will be described as probabilities, not certainties. It is worth noting that much of what you'll read about each type in low awareness can often still be considered strengths that help make the world go round. In fact, sometimes what keeps someone of a particular type from growing beyond their type's limitations is that their behaviors are often valuable strengths that are appreciated by others and even rewarded! As one who leads with Ennea-type Three, I can attest to the reality that America very much values the characteristics of Threes. In today's context, exacerbated by social media, there is a lot of pressure to be (or *appear* to be) successful at all costs. I've received some of my biggest attaboys in life when I was most engulfed in the trappings of my type. My outward success stands to be my inner demise. Transcending those tendencies for my own well-being means I may get far less applause in the future. I must learn not only to accept that but actually to prefer it.

The chapters ahead will hopefully help you to step onto the path of awareness with new discoveries and practical suggestions for growth. As you read, pay attention to the subtle, often-unconscious motivations and self-limiting stories that are playing just below the surface of the low-awareness descriptors you'll read about. Then imagine how much truer and more beautiful each type's expressions are in the high-awareness sections.

In higher levels of awareness, we reconnect to our inner depths. We are unrestricted by old belief systems. We are no longer fumbling around in the dark and trying to figure out who we are becoming because we have reconnected to what was dormant and have watched it come alive in us again. As Parker Palmer once wrote, "Our deepest calling is to grow into our own authentic selfhood, whether or not it conforms to some image of who we *ought* to be. As we do so, we will not only find the joy that every human being seeks—we will also find our path of authentic service in the world."[1]

This is what awareness is all about. This is emotional intelligence. And it's not something that some people are born with while the rest of us are doomed to stumble around, forever getting in our own way. It's something that is available to everyone. We just need to find our angel in the marble so we can set it free.

Let's get started.

PART 1

WHAT WE DON'T KNOW HURTS US

1

The Enneagram at a Glance

The Enneagram is much more demanding and much more dangerous than believing things. It is more about "unbelieving" the disguise that we all are.

Richard Rohr

Since you've picked up this book, you've likely heard of the Enneagram. If not, that's fine too. I've attempted to write this book in a way that will make sense to those who are new to the system as well as offer something more to those who may already know it quite well.

Wherever you are on the Enneagram knowledge spectrum, we are starting with this at-a-glance chapter just to make sure we are all looking at the same blueprint. Following is a brief overview for anyone who may not know much about the Enneagram and for those who learned the Enneagram years ago but may benefit from a high-level refresher before we get to the crux of our discussion.

The Symbol and the System

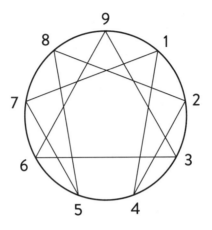

The Enneagram is an ancient discovery of nine core motivations and how they relate with one another. Some suggest that its roots can be traced as far back as the fourth century to Evagrius, a Christian contemplative (also known as one of the Desert Fathers) who analyzed which specific thoughts interfered with the meditative practices of each monk in his monastery. It is believed that he wrote about eight of these (which correspond to eight of the modern Enneagram types) but that many of his writings were destroyed by the church and labeled as heresy. Other people place the Enneagram's origins in later Sufi wisdom traditions.[1]

Whatever its origins in the distant past, the modern system we have today was developed through the works of twentieth-century pioneers such as George Gurdjieff, Oscar Ichazo, and the Chilean-born psychiatrist Claudio Naranjo. Since then, many others in the field of psychology have worked to further refine the Enneagram system. The system reveals nine personality archetypes and their underlying fears and desires. It tells us where we get stuck in overidentifying with one of the nine types and provides a map for us to move beyond archetypal patterns of our personality and self-limiting beliefs.

Identifying Your Type

The core type that you lead with is all about your unconscious strategies and underlying motivations. The Enneagram isn't focused on what you do but *why* you do it. Many types share similar interests and preferences but often for very different reasons. For example, a Three and a Five may both be high achieving, but the Three tends to do it to win admiration while the Five does it as part of an endless quest for expertise. Likewise, people of different Enneagram types may share the same or similar profiles on psychometrics like Myers-Briggs, yet the motivations and strategies behind their actions are unrelated.

The important thing to understand before we go any further is that *you aren't your type.* You are far more complex, wonderful, quirky, and nuanced than any type description could possibly encapsulate. We should not bother studying the Enneagram simply to learn a few new things about who we are. The long-term goal of learning our Ennea-type is to learn who we *aren't.*

The first thing to note is that you don't have a type—your type has you. Our personalities (Ennea-types) evolved in large part to protect us. They are masks we adopted to shield us from real or perceived threats and to get us closer to love and acceptance. We will explore this more in the next chapter, but I contend that the first reason so few people are truly self-aware is because they can't see past their own mask! Perhaps they know the mask so well that they've confused it with their truest essence, their most authentic self. They've been deceived into believing that the mask is real. As I told you in the introduction, I bought into this lie for much of my own life.

For a significant majority of those who've been shown the Enneagram, seeing their mask through the language of type becomes just another affirmation of the mask, a replication of the false self they have adopted. Instead, working with the Enneagram can teach you *why* the mask is there in the first place and provide guidance for slowly removing it.

We are made to contain all nine Ennea-types, and we do. But we entered the world with certain "factory settings" and then entered a personal childhood story that would test those settings and demand that they be adapted and adjusted in order for us to survive our circumstances. This led to an overidentification with the motivations and desires of one of these nine core types as our primary strategy for getting our needs met (on a mostly unconscious level) at the expense of being able to freely access the gifts of the other eight types. And although no one knows for sure, it's possible that our factory settings also included a particular sensitivity to the highest expression of our dominant Enneagram type, which went unmet in childhood. In other words, it's possible that we were born with the healthiest, highest expression of one of the nine types, but then that expression was crushed beneath the weight of a hurtful world. So we learned to take on the exact opposite characteristics of our truest selves, and our vision became clouded. Enneagram teacher and author Sandra Maitri described the impact like this: "The effect is that our particular unobstructed view of reality is weakened, diminished, and overshadowed by the vicissitudes of our formative years."[2]

For me, someone who identifies as a type Three, this could mean I entered the world resting in divine hope that I would be seen and loved for who I am, without conditions or expectations. My own feelings would be appreciated and validated, and I'd experience total acceptance. However, as I encountered the world around me with a sensitivity to these inborn needs, I internalized the opposite message: I would *not* be seen or loved for who I really was. Every time some well-meaning person told me to "just be yourself," it seemed to backfire spectacularly. No, what people really wanted was for me to be whomever would make their lives better, easier. The world values doers, and flawless doers at that! Over time, the part of me that came into the world valuing veracity above all else quietly put it away. I slowly learned to adapt to the subtle shifts in expectations from room to room, teacher to teacher, friend to friend, until I lost touch with myself. I was now whatever persona I needed to be, but I was completely unaware of the chameleon I'd become.

That impression I got about not being accepted for who I was has a name: it was a *wounding message.* As a Three, my wounding message was that I needed to constantly perform and exceed expectations, but each Ennea-type has its own wounding message. Identifying yours can be a key to unlocking which of the nine types best describes you.

Some tips for identifying your type include the following:

- Think back to all the watershed moments in your life: when you were faced with important decisions, when you felt anxious about something, or how you behaved when longing to experience love or have a particular need met. What was motivating you?
- Look for the number that best describes you, not the number you wish you were. (I'd love to be an energetic, healthy, and aware Seven, but I'm not.)
- Don't expect to identify with every single feature of any one type.
- If something about a certain type description makes you uncomfortable or irritable, lean into it. It's possible you are feeling that way because it's a negative trait that describes something you are denying about yourself.

Centers of Intelligence

As you think about which type you are, one helpful aspect of the Enneagram's system is to consider which of the three centers of intelligence that type is part of. The nine core Ennea-types take in information and make decisions by leaning most heavily on one of these three centers. A major part of the work ahead for each type is to bring the centers into greater balance by also starting to utilize the other two.

The gut center (Body types) is composed of types Eight, Nine, and One. These types seek to experience life through their senses. They tend to be concerned with matters of right versus wrong and are motivated to stand against injustice. The primary emotion sitting right below the surface for Body types is *anger*. Since they are concerned with issues of justice, much of this experience of anger is a posture of standing against whatever they see as unjust.

The feeling center (Heart types) is composed of types Two, Three, and Four. These types understand the world first and foremost through their emotions. They tend to be highly relational and are the most image-conscious of all the types. The primary emotion sitting right below the surface for Heart types is *sadness*. While many Enneagram practitioners teach that the primary emotion for Heart types is shame, through my study with the CP Enneagram Academy, I've come to believe that sadness is the common emotional thread and is a truer description. As they are preoccupied with how they are being perceived, much of their experience of sadness comes from being disconnected from their truest selves and from not feeling valued by others. Fours, for example, are prone to feelings of shame because of the false belief that they are flawed in some way, and Twos may feel shame when they ask someone directly to meet one of their own needs, but I think sadness is the common emotional thread between the Heart types.

Shame tends to be an embodied distress that any of the nine types may experience from a regrettable action. But much of what motivates the actions of Heart types in particular is the relentless pursuit of alleviating the sadness of not having been able to internalize unconditional affirmation of their inherent value as young people. Paradoxically, the generalized sadness only grows the more each Heart type tries to satiate it with their personality coping strategies since these schemes push them further from their truest selves—the very parts that were left invalidated in childhood and remain invalidated with every egoic attempt to fix them.

The thinking center (Head types) is composed of types Five, Six, and Seven. These types try to make sense of the world through thinking and logic. They tend to be "in their heads" much of the time, often planning and using their imaginations. The primary emotion sitting right below the surface for Head types is *fear*. Because they are concerned with wanting to be certain about things, they feel more fear than other types over what they cannot predict. This fear is also a manifestation of feeling far from their true selves.

We are made to have all three of these centers in balance, working harmoniously in each moment. In an ideal world, we'd be able to rely on whatever center of intelligence is most needed according to the situation in which we find ourselves. However, this is rarely the case. Each Ennea-type is dominant in one center, supported by a second center, while repressing the third. And the more out of balance we are, the more difficult it is to engage the world from a place of wholeness and awareness.

Passions and Virtues

Another important feature of the nine types discussed below is that each has a passion (vice)—whatever the self-delusion is for your particular Ennea-type—and a virtue. Although the passions for each Enneagram type are very different, their effect is the same. Think of the passion as being *overtaken*, like a crime of passion. The passion of each type completely consumes the authentic expression of the truer self (the Enneagram virtue) and runs our lives until we can no longer tolerate the pain it is causing us. In your early years, your type's passion probably helped you survive. Later in life, it may run you off the road.

And this is how all types get stuck. Each Ennea-type has its virtuous expression of God-given truth. As we live out our respective stories, our virtue gets wounded, and we begin to believe we're not safe to express it. Little by little, we learn to mask virtue with this thing we call "personality," and from then on the passion is in charge. The passion of our type is bigger and more all-consuming than you'll likely want to believe. But until we do the difficult work of getting unstuck, the passion controls us and not the other way around.

The chart below illustrates healthy thinking and emotional expression (virtue) for each Ennea-type in high awareness—that is, the true self. This is followed by the internalized wounding message that moves each type away from the virtue and to the emotional vice (passion)—that is, the false or adapted self.

Type	Healthy Thinking (Perceiving Reality)	Virtue (True Self)	Wounding Message	Passion (Adapted Self)
One	Accepting what is	Serenity	It's not okay to make mistakes.	Anger
Two	Recognizing one's own needs	Humility	Others' needs are more important than mine.	Pride
Three	Accepting the laws of creation	Authenticity	It's not okay to have my own feelings or identity.	Self-deception
Four	Knowing that nothing is missing	Equanimity	It's not okay to be too content in the world.	Envy
Five	Knowing my needs will be met	Nonattachment	It's not okay to be too comfortable in the world.	Avarice
Six	Faith that all will be okay	Courage	It's not okay to trust myself.	Fear
Seven	Knowing things are unfolding according to design	Sobriety	It's not okay to depend on anyone.	Gluttony
Eight	Understanding the all-inclusiveness of reality	Innocence	It's not okay to be vulnerable or trust others.	Lust
Nine	Perceiving the goodness of reality	Right action	It's not okay to assert myself.	Sloth

Fortunately, the Enneagram doesn't just show us our type's virtue and passion; it gives us a way to transcend the passion (adapted self) and reclaim the virtue (true self). As Ian Morgan Cron describes in his book *The Story of You*, "What separates the Enneagram from other personality typing systems is that it helps us craft and live a better, truer story than the one we've unconsciously settled for."[3]

Enneagram Type Descriptions

Type One

Core Theme: No one tries harder than Ones. They are focused, responsible, ethical, and trustworthy. They are motivated to achieve an ideal of perfection and value those who do the same.

They *instinctively* believe that they know what is right or wrong, good or bad, and they have a sense of mission that leads them to want to improve the world in various ways, using whatever degree of influence they have. They strive to overcome adversity—particularly moral adversity—so that the human spirit can shine through and make a difference. They strive after higher values, even at great personal cost. Although they have a strong sense of purpose, they also typically feel they have to justify their actions to themselves and often to others as well.

Core Motivation: To be above reproach in all things, continually improve the world around them, and achieve an ideal of perfection.

Wounding Message: "It's not okay to make mistakes."

Superpower: An unwavering commitment to high standards and impeccable quality. Ones have unshakable self-discipline, pushing themselves and others toward better and better outcomes.

Focus of Attention: Look for what is wrong and then to how it can be fixed or improved. Ones quickly categorize things into right and wrong.

Communication Style: Task-focused, precise, and filled with messages about an ideal picture of reality.

Physical Profile: Tends to be higher energy and busy with the tasks that need doing each day. May experience physical rigidity in the body, including a clenched jaw and an overall embodied resentment about the way things are.

Center of Intelligence: Body (types Eight, Nine, and One). *Anger* is the primary emotion associated with this center of intelligence.

How Ones Deal with Anger: By actively suppressing it. Ones want to be "good," which in their minds does not include succumbing to anger. They will sometimes channel their anger into righteous indignation over a cause but will otherwise tell themselves and others that they're not angry.

Passion: Anger

Virtue: Serenity

Type Two

Core Theme: Twos are natural servant leaders and willing friends who will often go to great lengths to help others succeed. They easily connect to the feelings of others and direct their attention toward being of service. They tend to concentrate on others' needs far more than their own. In fact, they can often lose themselves in people, finding their sense of identity through the approval of loved ones who give them a sense of importance. This is why they naturally focus on pleasing others as an unconscious strategy for being liked and accepted.

Helping and giving may be strategies Twos use in certain circumstances but not always. Their approach is often more subtle and seductive than that. The reason for pleasing or seducing is to avoid asking to have their needs met directly. To do that might result in an overt rejection, which would be heartbreaking. Being indirect helps Twos feel protected from the risk of explicit rejection.

Core Motivation: Twos are motivated by a need to be needed—to give love in order to get love.

Wounding Message: "Others' needs are more important than mine."

Superpower: Unflinching devotion to helping others thrive, bringing warmth and care to the people in their lives.

Focus of Attention: Look for particular people who Twos sense need help—even if the recipients themselves don't know it yet. May use flattery and unsolicited advice as a way to feel needed.

Communication Style: Concerned with people over tasks. Use a lot of feeling words while sending messages of support and advice.

Physical Profile: Often waiting with bated breath for important others to respond to them, thereby validating them. May experience significant tension in their chest.

Center of Intelligence: Heart (types Two, Three, and Four). *Sadness* is the primary emotion associated with this center of intelligence.

How Twos Deal with Sadness: By continually trying to please others through offering advice, help, and gifts. They seek confirmation of their value as a person through directing all of their emotional energy toward the needs of others in hopes of receiving validation back in the form of gratitude and compliments, which they mistakenly believe will alleviate their own sadness.

Passion: Pride

Virtue: Humility

Type Three

Core Theme: At the center of the Heart triad, Threes are actually the *most* feeling of all Ennea-types. However, believing their value lies in what they achieve, they actively repress their own feelings to stay focused on tasks and accomplishments.

In their hearts, Threes *feel* what others expect of them and then automatically become that expectation. They do this effortlessly and mechanically, becoming someone that they aren't to win admiration. Eventually, they will lose touch with their authentic selves—confusing the adapted self for the genuine. The biggest lie that Threes tell themselves, however, is that they aren't a feeling type—that they don't have very many emotions. In truth, Threes are *very* emotional.

Core Motivation: To feel valued through their accomplishments. To succeed, or at least appear successful, in all they do and avoid failure.

Wounding Message: "It's not okay to have my own feelings or identity."

Superpower: Driven to achieve tangible and noticeable results, Threes cast a brilliant vision for the future. Through charm and determination, they can persuade others to buy in and commit to delivering on important goals.

Focus of Attention: Immediately notice the desires, expectations, values, climate, clothing, and overall vibe of any room, and then automatically adapt to become the best representation of that environment.

Communication Style: Adaptive to the style of the audience. Goal- and task-oriented, Threes' communication is filled with messages and encouragement about the future.

Physical Profile: Often charismatic and exuding high energy. Threes may have difficulty sitting still or focusing on any one person for too long and are prone to "working the room." May avoid their feelings by directing their energy into goals. This can lead to a buildup of repressed emotion in the chest.

Center of Intelligence: Heart (types Two, Three, and Four). *Sadness* is the primary emotion associated with this center of intelligence.

How Threes Deal with Sadness: By disconnecting from their own emotions. Threes direct all their feelings outward to assess what others around them admire, then do their best to impress. Threes mask sadness through constant activities and pretending they are unemotional.

Passion: Self-deception

Virtue: Authenticity

Type Four

Core Theme: Fours are perhaps the most complex type. Without going into detail here, Fours can often mistype themselves if they don't readily identify with sadness or suffering, which is how Fours are usually described. However, depending on subtype, there are the sad Fours, the mad Fours, and the glad Fours (Social Fours, One-to-One Fours, and Self-Preservation Fours).[4]

Each type of Four shares an overidentification with suffering in one way or another. Fours see a world they don't feel they belong to. It's like they are peering in the window of your seemingly normal and wonderful life, longing to feel at home where you are but believing they are fatally flawed and will never be part of it. The constant comparisons they make in their minds cause them to set themselves apart and choose to be unique, pushing themselves further away from the thing that they want (belonging) by pretending that they don't want it. In this way, they may unconsciously sabotage the human connection they covet. They long to know and be known on a deep and meaningful level.

Core Motivation: To express their unique individuality and significance; to avoid the ordinary. Fours minister to their own emotions before tending to anything else.

Wounding Message: "It's not okay to be too content in the world."

Superpower: Emotionally intuitive and deeply committed to personal values. Can see behind any facade and, from a place of empathy, offer creative solutions in many challenging situations.

Focus of Attention: Fours are prone to adopting the aesthetics, metaphors, and feelings around them and therefore feel like something is missing from their present. Because they are comparing those things with an idealized version of past experiences, they long for a present that feels as special as their romanticized version of the past.

Communication Style: Creative, expressive, and inclined toward feeling words. May be self-referencing and overly focused on the negative.

Physical Profile: Energy can vacillate between lethargy and dramatic expressions. Emotions may sometimes feel like they are pooling in the chest, leading to experiences of anxiety and/or depression.

Center of Intelligence: Heart (types Two, Three, and Four). *Sadness* is the primary emotion associated with this center of intelligence.

How Fours Deal with Sadness: Often through creative expression. Whether through the arts, their vocation, choice of clothing, body modifications, or a myriad of other ways, Fours can usually connect deeply with sadness and are often gifted at turning it into beautiful outward messages for the world. If Fours can show people how special they are, they mistakenly believe it will finally alleviate the sadness.

Passion: Envy

Virtue: Equanimity

Type Five

Core Theme: Fives possess an amazing ability to observe and evaluate the interconnectedness of all things. They are contemplative, independent, and generally humble. They are usually very smart and intellectual to the point where they can sometimes be dismissive of information that comes from feelings (favored by Heart types) or instinctual knowledge (Body types).

Fives fear being overwhelmed by feeling, so they tend to talk about their feelings after the fact, as if they are analyzing the experience from a safe distance rather than experiencing the depth of their emotions in real time. This expression varies by subtype, but all Fives are predisposed to retreating into intellectual spaces.

Core Motivation: To be competent and knowledgeable, figuring things out as a way to feel certain and avoid being helpless, dependent, or overwhelmed.

Wounding Message: "It's not okay to be too comfortable in the world."

Superpower: Extremely observant with a gift for seeing the interrelation of most things. Can easily break things down into their component parts until they are fully understood. Capable of working independently.

Focus of Attention: Assessing who or what in the room may steal energy from them, then creating emotional buffers between themselves and those perceived threats.

Communication Style: Calm, rational, and analytical. Likely to listen more than speak except in safe environments when speaking about topics in which they have expertise.

Physical Profile: Up in their own heads—may appear "out to lunch" when looking in their eyes. Energetically limited and somewhat rigid, they lead with the head and the body follows after. They tend to dress simply and may not spend much time fussing over personal appearance.

Center of Intelligence: Head (types Five, Six, and Seven). *Fear* is the primary emotion associated with this center of intelligence.

How Fives Deal with Fear: By trying to understand and make sense of things. Fives withdraw from that which overwhelms them and use their isolation to contemplate and procure knowledge.

Passion: Avarice

Virtue: Nonattachment

Type Six

Core Theme: Every type fears certain things. Sixes simply fear. Their fear is more of a generalized anxiety about all possible risks that threaten their safety and the safety of those they love. This gets expressed in vastly different ways, depending on subtype, as there are both *phobic* and *counterphobic* versions of the Six (counterphobic Sixes often look like Eights as they tend to intensely confront the things that scare them in a semiconscious attempt to overcome their fears). They are delightfully contrarian verbal processors. They think out loud a lot as they try to work out all possible risks. Sometimes what they say aloud isn't even what they really think—it's just the contrarian point of view they need to say in order to see if they believe it. This is how they approach problem-solving.

Sixes are one of the most loyal types and are steadfast supporters of those they deem reliable, responsible, and as trustworthy as they are.

Core Motivation: To feel secure and supported by others, and to pursue certitude in all things that may affect them.

Wounding Message: "It's not okay to trust myself."

Superpower: Uncanny ability to anticipate risks, question assumptions, and challenge ideas. Deeply loyal, wonderful team members who are often very calm in an actual crisis because they've already anticipated it.

Focus of Attention: Scanning for potential hazards and threats in order to prepare for anything that might go wrong.

Communication Style: Tend to ask a lot of questions and process their concerns aloud, often playing devil's advocate to any and all ideas. Usually transparent and direct with their words.

Physical Profile: Fight-or-flight. When presented with conflict, phobic Sixes tend to physically and/or mentally withdraw, while counterphobic Sixes go up against the thing that scares them with strength and aggression. Both types of Sixes tend to carry tension in their muscles and may exhibit shallow breathing patterns.

Center of Intelligence: Head (types Five, Six, and Seven). *Fear* is the primary emotion associated with this center of intelligence.

How Sixes Deal with Fear: By questioning things. Sixes may also overidentify with certain authority figures and/or belief systems as a way to feel safe, or they may doubt and reject authority and choose to go up against their fears head-on.

Passion: Fear

Virtue: Courage

Type Seven

Core Theme: Sevens can bring joy to any room and are fantastic at helping us all to remember how important it is to celebrate our successes. They tend to be future-focused, imaginative, and enthusiastic innovators.

As a Head type, Sevens are attempting to deal with the primary emotion of fear—specifically, the fear of suffering. So they choose optimism. This can lead them to perpetually reframe negatives into positives (often by looking only at data that confirms their views and avoiding data that doesn't) and then quickly move on to the next big thing that will help them live the good life.

Core Motivation: A drive to experience all interesting possibilities, to be stimulated and content, and to avoid limitations.

Wounding Message: "It's not okay to depend on anyone."

Superpower: Highly energized, future-focused optimism that can bring out the passion and fun in any team they're part of. Fantastic brainstormers and storytellers.

Focus of Attention: Hunting for all possible opportunities for enhancing novelty while also avoiding or ignoring limitations.

Communication Style: Future-oriented, expressive, charming, and often in the form of stories. Sevens usually avoid sad topics.

Physical Profile: Sevens move away from uncomfortable feelings by being up in their heads. They struggle to remain grounded and present in their own bodies. They often radiate a contagious exuberance for life.

Center of Intelligence: Head (types Five, Six, and Seven). *Fear* is the primary emotion associated with this center of intelligence.

How Sevens Deal with Fear: By trying to outrun and out-fun fear. Sevens use planning, dreaming, and reframing negatives as ways to avoid their fears and negative feelings. Their often-contagious energy and enthusiasm make it difficult to see any fear in this type at all.

Passion: Gluttony

Virtue: Sobriety

Type Eight

Core Theme: Eights are sometimes known as the Challengers because, out of all the types, they enjoy taking charge as well as challenging others. Eights have more energy than any other type on the Enneagram. They are often charismatic and possess the ability to persuade others to follow them.

Eights are fiercely independent. They have enormous willpower and vitality, and they use their abundant energy to effect changes in the world—often very positive changes that are concerned with justice and injustice. They desire to leave their mark on the world and protect the people they love, keeping them safe from harm.

Core Motivation: Driven by a need to be strong, self-reliant, and in control of their own destiny.

Wounding Message: "It's not okay to be vulnerable or trust others."

Superpower: Decisive doers who make things happen. Filled with passion, Eights are willing to step up, speak up, and take charge.

Focus of Attention: Matters of fairness, justice, and urgency. They home in on who has the most power in the room and assess how well they are wielding that power. If Eights aren't satisfied with how others are leading, they may take over.

Communication Style: Direct, clear, and assured. Often tend toward all-or-nothing messages.

Physical Profile: Intense and quick to anger. Tend toward a posture of appearing bigger than they are, full of bodily energy and tension.

Center of Intelligence: Body (types Eight, Nine, and One). *Anger* is the primary emotion associated with this center of intelligence.

How Eights Deal with Anger: Openly. Eights have no problem acting on their anger and may view it as something that brings them energy. They aren't afraid of conflict and will sometimes even seek it out.

Passion: Lust

Virtue: Innocence

Type Nine

Core Theme: Wonderful, democratic consensus builders, Nines sit atop the Enneagram diagram, symbolically representing their vantage point as people who can truly sense what it's like to be each of the other Ennea-types. This includes empathy but not so much from the heart—it's a *knowing* in the gut what it is like to walk in another's shoes. This enables them to excel in diplomacy, but it can also be a liability, as Nines can sometimes be indecisive and unwilling to lead or act.

Nines are generally easy to work with because of their thoughtful, considerate ways. However, they tend to minimize their own importance and get stuck in routines as a tactic to avoid acting on their own personal agendas. But since they also don't want other people's agendas to control them, they can tend toward passive-aggressive behavior (which is how they deal with the underlying anger they are trying to avoid experiencing).

Core Motivation: Driven by a desire to be settled, avoid conflict, and resist what would disrupt their sense of peace and harmony.

Wounding Message: "It's not okay to assert myself."

Superpower: Seeing the world from multiple perspectives. Nines are naturally supportive team players who bring a sense of calm to the room. They are caring and attentive.

Focus of Attention: Being agreeable. Nines will quietly listen for the opportunity for consensus and then merge with the desires of others. They may struggle to believe that their presence matters, making themselves less noticeable through passive acquiescence.

Communication Style: Inclusive, amicable, friendly, and other-focused. They're unlikely to offer an opinion unless asked directly.

Physical Profile: Unhurried, even idle. Nines tend to be lower energy and often have problems with inertia. They may store in their bodies the tension and conflict they avoid in their day-to-day interactions.

Center of Intelligence: Body (types Eight, Nine, and One). *Anger* is the primary emotion associated with this center of intelligence.

How Nines Deal with Anger: By ignoring it. Since Nines understand their role in life as being peacemakers, they often aren't aware of their own anger. It may build up inside them and then emerge in passive-aggressive ways.

Passion: Sloth

Virtue: Right action

2

Emotional Intelligence

The curious paradox is that when I accept myself just as I am, then I can change.

Carl R. Rogers

Marty was a successful entrepreneur. In a relatively short time, he amassed a small personal fortune and made a name for himself within elite circles of other like-minded business leaders. Soon after selling his company and enjoying a brief early retirement, Marty was asked to join a fledgling organization as their new CEO. The board was sure that Marty's proven track record of past success was predictive evidence of his ability to fix their problems and scale their business.

As an entrepreneur, Marty had created, developed, and delivered a wildly popular business solution. He had operated in nearly total autonomy, made all the decisions, executed quickly, and removed any obstacles with force. As a new CEO, he attempted to do the exact same thing that had made him so successful. He operated autonomously without involving the experts in the organization. He held weekly meetings with his direct reports but frequently made decisions he believed were best despite any evidence to support them and without really listening to his closest advisers. He acted rashly on everything from changing company branding to changing external partnerships and did all of this with a force that rendered perceptions of him throughout the organization as uninformed, unapproachable, and unhelpful. Marty would eventually leave his post after a series of resignations from important experts on the team, disengagement from the remaining staff, and a faltering reputation in the communities in which they operated.

Daniel earned multiple degrees, including a PhD in organizational leadership. He was a salt-of-the-earth kind of guy with a heart as big as his student debt. Daniel functioned as a general manager of his organization, and when the incoming president met Daniel for the first time, he was certain he struck gold to have a leader with such an impressive educational background as his number two. But Daniel frequently disappointed the new president and eventually had to leave. It was a particularly sad departure, as everyone in the organization really liked Daniel. He had spent the bulk of each week of his employment meeting with people and cultivating relationships. He was quick to invite anyone to lunch but painfully slow in making decisions or delivering on commitments. Daniel was so afraid of making a wrong decision in his role that he neglected to make decisions at all. Instead of debating with the president over the best way to take a project forward, he would passively imply agreement but fail to deliver on expectations. Daniel prioritized interpersonal relationships at the expense of all else. No amount of coaching helped because he already knew the answers. More information wasn't needed, more doing was. Unfortunately, he just couldn't close the gap between knowing and doing.

These are but two tales of everyday failures by well-intended, well-educated, and well-established individuals who on paper had every reason to succeed—but didn't. These two seemingly opposite personalities crashed for the same reason: they lacked self-awareness.

Self-awareness enables people to do things others simply can't. People with high awareness have greater optionality because they observe and understand more than others do. Both Marty and Daniel lacked the capacity for behavioral change because, despite all their expertise, they were without an embodied sense of self. Without an embodied awareness, the only real choice they had available to them was to double down on past strategies while scratching their heads as to why it wasn't working. Time and again, people like Marty and Daniel are hired for what they know and fired for who they are. And it's not because there is something wrong with who they are; it's because they are completely unaware of who they are, what's truly going on inside, and the effect it has on everyone around them. They are emotionally unintelligent.

A Working Definition of Emotional Intelligence

I often hear the topic of emotional intelligence discussed in social and organizational circles, and I'm sometimes struck by a notion that perhaps we aren't all talking about the same thing. It seems to me that in many instances the term *emotional intelligence* has almost become synonymous for how we think about people we like and people we don't. If I get along well with you and you don't get in my way or bother me, I say you are a person with high emotional intelligence. If, on the other hand, you are a challenge for me to work with, I don't often agree with your opinions, or I can't understand your feelings, I might describe you as having low emotional intelligence.

These internal reactions, of course, are not reliable indications of other people's emotional intelligence. In fact, they often depict our own low emotional intelligence because we are allowing a lifetime of often unprocessed personal feelings to determine our opinions of others according to our own preferences and biases. We misinterpret such feelings as confirmation of the personal beliefs we already hold and are then quite pleased to carry on as if we understand the other person or situation perfectly. The stronger the feeling, the more certain we become that we are right.

So let's start with a working definition of *emotional intelligence* (which I will also refer to as EQ). Emotional intelligence is a measure of how effective we are at continually accessing, understanding, managing, and leveraging our emotions in our day-to-day relationships with ourselves and others. There are varied descriptions of this idea, and many scholarly papers and books explain the nuances of emotional intelligence in much greater detail. But for our purposes, having a high EQ involves understanding the interplay of our feelings, thoughts, and actions. It is a cultivated ability to continually ask ourselves, *What is going on in my heart, my head, and my body?* In this chapter, we'll talk about why we naturally struggle to have a consistently high EQ, even though our ability to develop our EQ is the single biggest predictor of our personal and professional success.

RAISING AWARENESS

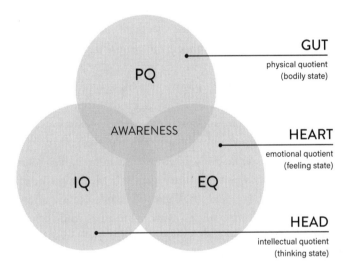

GUT
physical quotient
(bodily state)

PQ

AWARENESS

HEART
emotional quotient
(feeling state)

IQ   EQ

HEAD
intellectual quotient
(thinking state)

I am convinced that the first mistake many of us make when it comes to emotional intelligence is that we assume we already know ourselves and others. On a fundamental level, nothing could be further from the truth (at least not until we do the work of developing this capability). Awareness is not binary, of course—we are all on a sliding scale of awareness about ourselves and others. But if you assume that you're high on these scales, there's a decent chance the opposite may be true. Keep in mind, nobody thinks they are emotionally unintelligent or completely lacking in self-awareness. Yet, as we will soon see, emotional intelligence is easy to understand and difficult to achieve. And self-awareness . . . well, the data on that is quite sobering (which we'll come to in a moment).

Our level of self-awareness and awareness of others as well as our ability to understand our emotions and respond productively in every situation form the foundation of emotional intelligence. Emotional intelligence, in turn, is the cornerstone of healthy relationships, organizations, and thriving communities and cultures. The higher our awareness, the greater our clarity. The clearer we are, the more capable we are to navigate the world, be happy, and bring out the best in ourselves and others.

The Importance of Awareness

Since the early 1990s, there has been escalating dialogue and research in the field of emotional intelligence. Various books, magazine articles, lectures, and workshops have explored the importance of EQ in leadership and beyond, recommending strategies for developing your emotional intelligence profile. If you think the discussion is overplayed, consider what research is telling us about how crucial EQ is for thriving individuals and organizations. Emotional intelligence, it turns out, is the single biggest predictor of success—of far greater importance than IQ. Research has shown that more than 70 percent of the reasons behind high performance are EQ related.[1] The data also shows that 75 percent of the reasons careers get derailed are EQ related.[2]

According to research conducted by organizational psychologist Tasha Eurich, author of *Insight*, "Senior executives who lack self-awareness are 600 percent more likely to derail (which can cost companies a staggering $50 million per executive)." Eurich concludes, "There is strong scientific evidence that people who know themselves and how others see them are happier. They make smarter decisions." She goes on to list several more compelling reasons why developing our awareness is essential to the whole of our lives, both personally and professionally. Yet self-awareness is absent much of the time. Eurich's research concluded that 95 percent of people believe they are self-aware, but only 10 to 15 percent of people actually are.[3]

Leaders with developed awareness can help create emotionally intelligent work cultures in which people will perform better. When an organization is emotionally intelligent, it is healthy— meaning that it creates the conditions necessary for everyone to maximize their discretionary effort. This is often referred to as *engagement*, meaning that employees feel motivated, committed, and psychologically safe to speak up, ideate, and contribute. Engagement isn't merely nice to have either. The data is clear that when people are engaged in their work, they improve profitability. In a global study of fifty thousand employees, the Corporate Leadership Council found that those who are fully engaged perform 20 percent better than those who are not as committed. Not only do these engaged employees perform their own duties more capably, but they also help their colleagues with their workloads, raise their hands for new projects, and continually identify ways in which the work can be done better.[4]

In another study, the Corporate Executive Board concluded that every 10 percent improvement in an individual's engagement increases their effort by 6 percent, which on average produces an increase in results by 2 percent. They called it the 10:6:2 Rule. This means that for a revenue-generating role, someone could generate 2 percent *more* revenue than they currently do just by increasing their engagement (commitment) by 10 percent.[5] That is significant!

This data isn't new, and it is already well understood by many organizations. I'm sure most leaders are well-intentioned in trying to hire and develop fully committed individuals to drive thriving organizational cultures and deliver maximum value. Yet most organizations would likely concede that they haven't reached their engagement goals. What then is the disconnect? Why is creating highly emotionally intelligent cultures that maximize employee commitment so difficult for even the best organizations to achieve?

The reasons are multifaceted and complex because such cultures include important organizational design elements, proper workforce planning, committed diversity and inclusion practices, organizational purpose, social responsibility, learning and development tools, career opportunities, and other factors. (For our purposes, we won't attempt to directly address any of these in this book, but what we will be addressing *does* indirectly affect each of these important elements.) But there is an elephant in the room that we will attempt to tackle, and here it is: we are not all motivated by the same things.

This is why trying to motivate others often fails—your team is made up of different individuals with fundamentally different motivations. In fact, according to Enneagram theory, there are at least nine primary differences in what motivates people. And among those nine primary motivational differences, there are at least twenty-seven variations (Enneagram subtypes). Within the twenty-seven variations, there are as many different expressions of those motivations as there are people on the planet. And here's the kicker: much of what motivates a person is unknown to them (at least at the conscious level). So how on earth can a leader, an organization, or a colleague automatically know how to motivate people who are fundamentally disconnected from what their own motivations are?

Honestly, they can't.

But here's what we *can* do. We can cultivate comprehensive self-awareness by getting in touch with our own unconscious motivations and blind spots. We can help nurture thriving cultures and communities by learning all we can about ourselves while compassionately supporting others to learn all they can about themselves. And we can all help one another by committing ourselves to exploring our inner depths in order to live more honest lives. Through the discipline of self-discovery, we have the opportunity to reconnect with our authentic personhood—our often-hidden desires, repressed emotions, unmet needs, and the self-limiting stories that interfere with our ability to be our best selves.

Normalizing the Language of Emotion

Building a healthy EQ profile requires integrating all the facets of our lives—from the personal to the professional. As long as we attempt to use feeling language with our friends and families while trying to use only professional language at work, we compartmentalize parts of ourselves that were never meant to be separated. Surfacing and constructively expressing our feelings doesn't interfere with our professionalism. Feelings are, in actuality, a profound source of insight that should be understood and leveraged in productive ways to fuel our creativity, decision-making, relationships, and communication. Part of our growth work is to learn to step into the language of emotion in every facet of our lives, particularly in our workplaces, as a source of relational and informational currency.

In reality, of course, it is still a challenge in many work environments to use feeling words other than passive banalities such as "good" or "fine" when asked, "How are you doing?" But high-performing organizations create cultures where feeling language and regular practices of personally checking in with each other are not only encouraged but expected. My friend and leadership expert Jean Gomes believes that's because high-performing cultures know that when we take the time to identify what we are feeling, we are much more likely to process that emotion and re-engage our prefrontal cortex to make clearer, smarter decisions throughout the workday. Our emotional state informs our cognitive capability and capacity.

Up until this point, we've been framing emotional intelligence primarily in the context of organizational life. But the purpose behind this book is much greater than that. We bring our whole selves to our work each and every day. Some do it consciously and positively influence the culture; some do it unconsciously and wreak havoc. Most of us do both. So forget what you may have been told about work/life balance being the key to happiness or how you must leave your feelings at the door when you enter the office or any of the thinking that states your personal life is personal and your professional life is professional, each closed off by some invisible line. This mindset pits one important thing against the other and diminishes our ability to treat all the important things in our lives as significant. In today's rapidly changing world, amid technological advancements and the ongoing evolution of the workplace, it's time to shift our mindset from the notion of work/life balance to work/life integration.

When our values are integrated, we become integrated. That's not to suggest we don't need boundaries, of course. In fact, fully integrating our lives means we must place clear boundaries around the resources that keep us functioning at optimal levels. For example, now you may be able to work wherever or whenever, which allows for you to integrate both personal and professional elements throughout your day. However, if you start bringing your laptop to bed, you're going to disrupt your sleep cycles and turn your bedroom into another work space. Your bedroom would serve you better if it remained device-free. Boundaries aren't limitations—they are enablers. They create the space we need to succeed. Without them, our lives become chaos.

Building Awareness

Our emotions are an undeniable source of insight. The problems come when we deny and repress them—dismissing them as less important than logic and reasoning. This strategy is shortsighted because emotions can never be ignored for long. Sooner or later, they will come out sideways and cause unintended damage. Building awareness, then, is to become more conscious of what we are feeling inside and the effect of our environment on our bodies. When we deny ourselves the chance to consciously engage with our feelings, we become less aware and experience emotional repression. Repressed emotions can grow to a disproportionate size until the next thing you know, you're yelling at your kids, arguing with your partner over something meaningless, or engaging in unhealthy coping behaviors in an attempt to keep your discomfort at bay. It's much better to give emotions opportunities to surface and to decipher their meaning while you still have a chance to do so in constructive ways.

Understanding our feelings can be helped by the growing body of neuroscience discovery and research that is upending the classical understanding of how emotions are constructed. These new understandings are reshaping how we understand emotional intelligence. As psychology professor Lisa Feldman Barrett writes, "You feel what your brain believes."[6] This area of neuroscience is revealing that many of our beliefs are informed by our brain's interpretation of constant sensory perceptions in the body, which are sent as signals to the brain through a process known as interoception.[7]

The developing understanding of how the interoceptive process works affirms what the Enneagram has revealed since it was first discovered—namely, that the body is as valuable a source of intelligence as our cognition and our emotions. All three systems—which the Enneagram refers to as Gut, Heart, and Head—are at work in us. And all three need to be brought back into balance so that we are no longer overreliant on the one that we prefer but can instead use all of them as needed.

Our bodily sensations influence our emotions profoundly. Becoming more aware of the way our physical sensations, emotions, and beliefs interact helps us to make better sense of the world and ourselves. Our brains largely run on predictions—assumptions based on past experiences—that interrelate with our senses. When prediction and sensory input (vision, hearing, physical feeling, etc.) align, we are calm and generally at peace. When they don't, our feelings represent an error signal, and we notice that something is amiss. If the error signal is big—say we become painfully embarrassed in a meeting because we are caught not knowing something—our body reacts milliseconds in advance, mobilizing fight-or-flight reactions. Our body knows first. So a way to interpret these feelings is to recognize that one of our real, perceived, or assumed needs isn't being met—in this case, the need for social safety.

When emotions arise in us, we must fully *feel* them so we can then turn our attention to any underlying beliefs or assumptions we carry that have created them. The stronger the negative feeling, the further we are from having one of our core needs met.

Whether you're an employee, a leader, a consultant, a homemaker, a pastor, or anything else, the outcomes of your life will be disproportionately dependent upon your ability to understand, process, and act on your emotions with thoughtful intentionality and regular consideration of the impact you have on others. As you will see, doing this well doesn't primarily come from a class or a book but from learning to recover your own emotional wholeness—to live a fully awakened, integrated life. This may seem bold to say to a reader I've likely never met and whose life circumstances I couldn't possibly know, but your emotional intelligence is predicated on your emotional healing. Your emotional intelligence is going to be the foundation of your future success in life and relationships. So how can you know whether you are emotionally intelligent and what areas need the most attention?

Measuring Emotional Intelligence

There are varied approaches to defining and measuring emotional intelligence, but they're each attempting to get at the same general result. For our purposes, we will be guided by the five EQ composite scales that I use in my coaching practice via the EQ-i 2.0 system.[8] These reports measure

1. Self-perception
2. Self-expression
3. Interpersonal relationships
4. Decision-making
5. Stress management

When someone comes to me for coaching, I give them an EQ self-assessment test and then go over the data with them. This gives them a chance to ask questions about their results as we look for patterns, imbalances, and so on. When a person is comparatively high in one area and low in another, that's an imbalance. If it is causing a pattern of unwanted outcomes or general personal struggle, I work with the individual to establish a plan for how to bring these imbalances into greater equilibrium.

The theory is that when you are made aware of your strengths and weaknesses, you can use that awareness to begin to develop your personal and interpersonal intelligence. Yet in my EQ-coaching work, I've seen some aha moments without much transformational change as reported by those I've coached (this could be one reason why there is some debate in the field as to whether EQ can actually be developed). I believe wholeheartedly that the report is measuring the right types of things and that there are many great EQ coaches who are asking the right follow-up questions and giving good advice. So what is the problem? Can emotional intelligence *really* be developed?

I believe it can. The problem is that knowing the problem isn't the same thing as solving the problem. Being made aware isn't *becoming* aware. In other words, seeing a report about where you have struggles probably isn't news to you. In fact, most people whose reports I debrief tell me they aren't surprised about any of it, no matter the results. They already know where there is low self-regard or challenges with managing stress or expressing themselves appropriately in a manner consistent with their best intentions. The report has confirmed for them what they already know or *think* they know about themselves—after all, these assessments are you according to you! You're asked a series of questions, and you answer them according to what you think about yourself. But what if you don't *really* know yourself? Have you then answered these questions correctly? And if you already did know all these things about yourself prior to seeing the report, why haven't you been able to change the unwanted parts already?

There are few surprises in any of the you-according-to-you psychometric inventories. Why? Because they don't sufficiently uncover the fears, desires, wounding messages, and self-limiting beliefs that are hidden from our view. These reports, along with revelations from most any other psychometric tool, can generate temporary awareness, but that doesn't fundamentally create the capacity for meaningful transformation. In fact, knowing our EQ scores may actually cause us to delay the real work we need to do because we confuse knowing with doing (just as Daniel did in this chapter's opening story). What's worse, using EQ measures alone may even cause our EQ to drop because there's a proclivity to get stuck in self-focus to the exclusion of all else.[9] We can't exactly develop high interpersonal skills, demonstrate empathy, manage stress, and make good decisions if we are consumed with thinking about ourselves. If we become myopic in our quest for self-awareness, we risk becoming self-absorbed.

True self-awareness is comprehensive—it is not simply how accurately you think you know yourself. You may have said or heard someone say, "He/she just doesn't understand me! I'm NOT like how they said I am." But this is not comprehensive self-awareness, which includes both *intrinsic* and *extrinsic* vantage points. Intrinsic self-awareness is to be conscious of and connected to your own personal values and desires and to live authentically in accordance with those values and aspirations. Extrinsic self-awareness is to be conscious of and connected to how other people perceive you and the impact of your behavior on everyone and everything around you. To possess comprehensive self-awareness is to see yourself clearly from every vantage point and then act accordingly.

Wherever you are on the scale of awareness at this very moment, I suspect there are times when you feel disconnected from yourself—that something is off with your self-perception or self-regard. Or perhaps at times you express yourself in a way that upsets someone or leaves you feeling misunderstood. Is there a relationship in your life that is wounded? Or do you feel overwhelmed with stress in today's world and worry about the types of decisions you're making?

Whatever your internal reactions are to these questions, you have an opportunity to radically transform both your intrinsic and extrinsic self-awareness. You can learn to surface all of your hidden parts and blind spots and move beyond what you already think you know. That's because a healthy emotional intelligence profile isn't attained by directly focusing on developing your emotional intelligence but in learning how to access what is unconscious in you. And in the process, you learn to lay down your defenses, surrender your fears, reconnect to the deepest parts of yourself, and recover your emotional wholeness. If you can do that, you may never need to read another article on emotional intelligence again.

Moving toward Emotional Wholeness

As you read this book, please do your best to be open and lean in. My sincere hope is that you will discover something you didn't realize about yourself and the people you live and work with every day in order to have richer, more productive relationships with more satisfying outcomes.

There are many typology systems, psychometrics, and personal inventory tools that can help us gain greater clarity about our personalities and behaviors. I employ many of these tools in the work that I do with individuals, teams, and leaders. However, there is no better tool I know for self-discovery and truly raising our awareness than the Enneagram. Most other systems are intellectual frameworks that don't translate into doing. But the Enneagram is a model of the head, heart, and body that helps us learn how to connect to our feelings and reintegrate all parts of ourselves. It is an embodied approach to understanding ourselves and others. That is why I'm using the Enneagram as our guide for learning how to truly, and finally, elevate our emotional profiles in meaningful and sustainable ways.

Every worthwhile journey to exciting new places requires a map, and the Enneagram provides one. If we take this journey, we will gain knowledge and wisdom beyond the thinking that got us stuck to begin with. It won't be easy. Going to a new place always means leaving somewhere more familiar. And fundamental to each of our own fragile ego structures is a desire to believe that we do not need to take the journey—that we don't actually have blind spots (other people do). We may insist that we already see ourselves clearly and that we understand our own behaviors and their impact on others perfectly well. Some of this thinking is rooted in a need to have a positive self-image. Some of it is because we are comfortable with the way things are, even if we're not particularly satisfied. However, if we want to be truly healthy, whole, and successful, we need to have a comprehensive view of everything—the beautiful parts *and* the broken parts.

We will be looking at emotional intelligence through the lenses of the five EQ measurements I discussed earlier: self-perception, self-expression, interpersonal relationships, decision-making, and stress management. Along the way, I'll be overlaying each of the nine primary Enneagram types onto these attributes to see how each type might naturally embody or struggle with a particular trait and what the implications are. When any one of these emotional intelligence scales gets out of sync with the others, they all suffer. For example, if we have too much stress in our lives and are struggling to cope, our decision-making abilities will be diminished. Or if I don't perceive myself, or you, with accuracy, our interpersonal relationship will become strained. And if our relationships are broken, our capacity for coping with stress is weakened. In other words, these measures are all interdependent.

But beyond the universal truths of our common EQ goals are unique and complex layers of superpowers belonging to each of the nine Enneagram types. When understood, these gifts have the power to unlock not only emotional intelligence in ourselves but also brilliance in others. As you delve into the chapters ahead, I hope you will begin to see each Ennea-type's particular approach to matters of emotional intelligence—fueled by its own factory settings and combined with layers of personal stories, childhood messages, unmet needs, core fears, hidden desires, and unconscious beliefs and motivations that show up in the world in a variety of both helpful and not-so-helpful ways.

As we get under the hood of each Enneagram type, we are going to highlight the core belief of each type and how those beliefs inform our thinking, seeing, and behaving. But before we begin, I want to acknowledge that beliefs are complex and come to us from several different sources. Many beliefs stem from messages we received from explicit family and cultural dynamics. Some are the product of a significant trauma that shaped our view of the world, independent of our personality type. Common to all beliefs, however, is an internalized hope that "this is how I will make sense of the world and get my needs met." Often, what is running the show are the wounding messages we internalized early in our stories that are blocking us from fully becoming the people we desire to be.

As you read on, please know that I'm describing each type in terms of probabilities, not absolutes. Nothing is always true of any one type, and I don't care much for generalities. Also, please note that the fastest way to make progress in learning about yourself through the lens of the Enneagram is for the Enneagram teacher to not shy away from talking about the shadow sides of our personalities. However, while there's a lot herein that may not be flattering, none of it is meant to be condemning or accusatory. I highlight some difficult-to-face possibilities precisely because much of the time that's the stuff we've been avoiding but is exactly what will help us create the greatest shifts. The Enneagram isn't a system designed for flattery, but it is intended to raise awareness in the most compassionate and empathetic ways possible. To that end, I will do my best to present even the most difficult truths with the compassion you deserve and the genuine love I feel for each of the nine core Ennea-types.

PART 2

RAISING OUR AWARENESS

3

Self-Perception

It is amazing how you can look in a mirror your whole life and think you are seeing yourself clearly. And then one day, you peel off a filmy gray layer of hypocrisy, and you realize you've never truly seen yourself at all.

Jodi Picoult

We all tell stories about ourselves. For the most part, the stories stay inside our heads, unspoken, but these narratives are powerful. Some of us hold a positive story, and some of us hold a cruel and self-defeating one. Either way, the story we tell about ourselves informs the story we write about others, the world, and how life works. These stories even dictate what we accomplish and what we do not.

Sometimes we are the overcomer in our own story, someone who does the impossible and is fueled by a strong belief in ourselves. This story says, "Yes, I can!" Other times we are the impostor or side character, the one with chronic bad luck fueled by a lack of self-confidence. This story says, "I am not enough."

Emotional intelligence is not about willpower but about healthy self-perception and understanding what is truly going on inside of us. Our goal isn't simply to conjure positivity with false optimism such as "If you believe it, you can achieve it!" When we are healthy and aware, we no longer see a conjured story about ourselves but the truth of who we are, including our shadow sides—the very parts that need empathy, compassion, and healing. We will find emotional intelligence when we find emotional wholeness, and wholeness starts with unedited personal acknowledgment.

A young woman who leads with type Two on the Enneagram once told me that every time she had a break from her grueling undergrad schoolwork, she'd visit her family. At some point during her stay she would, inevitably, look for an opportunity to surprise her family by cleaning the entire house or doing some big organizing project for them. When her family returned home from work, they would lavish her with appreciation for the unexpected gift. The praise she received fueled a belief that her greatest value was in serving others, and every "thank you" affirmed her value.

However, as she learned more about the trappings of her Ennea-type, combined with some helpful professional counseling, she eventually came to realize that her family never needed or expected her to take on all that work for them when she was supposed to be resting. All they really wanted was for her to have a soft place to land between semesters and to just enjoy having her around—not for what she might do for them but just for who she is. This shift in her self-perception—seeing that she was loved and needed without having to lift a finger—had a profound impact on her recovery and renewal while on breaks, which gave her the resources she needed to excel in her studies when it was time to return to dorm life.

In this chapter, we're diving into the first of the five building blocks of emotional intelligence: self-perception. How we view ourselves directly informs the way we behave and interpret the world. From an emotional intelligence perspective, self-regard is the cornerstone of well-being, effectiveness, and overall happiness. If we want to truly grow in emotional intelligence, we must ask ourselves, Is my self-perception accurate? I'll give you a hint: unless you see yourself like the new parent beholding their newborn—filled with wonder, love, and gratitude—then you do not see yourself accurately. The parent-to-infant relationship is one of attunement.[1] The good mother conveys to the infant, "You are loved. You are safe." And the good father's gaze communicates, "You are remarkable. You can do it. I believe in you."

This is not to suggest that accurate self-perception means ignoring our flaws or seeing ourselves with bias. It is, instead, recognizing that the first step toward an honest perception of ourselves is through the eyes of compassionate self-love and acceptance. When we see ourselves through the eyes of our egos, we will either aggrandize or self-criticize, both of which will lead us to hide away important parts of ourselves—the former for the sake of pride, the latter because of shame. The only way we can truly learn to see ourselves more accurately is through attuning to the deepest truths of who we are—worthy of love, safe to be who we are, remarkable, and capable of growth.

Enneagram Types and Self-Perception

The following is a look at the nine core Enneagram types and what self-perception may look like when each type is in an unhealthy space (low self-awareness) and a healthy space (high self-awareness). Each type has its own customary traps of false belief as well as a path toward a truer, more accurate self-perception—which is the first trait we need in order to develop our emotional intelligence. As you read, you'll notice that the difference between low and high self-awareness is the difference in the stories we tell ourselves about ourselves.

Type One

In **low awareness**, Ones' self-perception can be one of the lowest of all Ennea-types. We all have an inner critic, but for those who lead with type One, their inner critic is often an ensemble cast. They believe they instinctively know what is right or wrong, good or bad. And they constantly evaluate themselves and others on how successful—or more often, how unsuccessful—they are at living up to those impossibly high black-and-white standards. Ones can get so busy beating themselves up that they become blind to their own innate goodness. Their skewed self-perception magnifies every flaw and discounts every strength.

In **high awareness**, Ones move away from comparing themselves to the impossible standard of perfection and begin to see themselves through a more realistic and compassionate lens. They more readily accept the flaws in themselves and others. In this way, they improve their self-perception, not because they've improved themselves but because they've stopped believing that they need to be perfect to be considered "good."

Type Two

In **low awareness**, Twos believe they are unworthy of love and acceptance if they aren't explicitly feeling needed by other people. Paradoxically, they may simultaneously be filled with a pride that they, and only they, know the best way to help someone else or solve organizational problems. This can produce a mixed result because both pride and shame are equally in charge. In lower levels of awareness, Twos are the most codependent of all the Ennea-types. Their self-perception fluctuates dramatically from moment to moment since their senses of worth and well-being are so closely tied to how others respond to them.

In **high awareness**, Twos' need for external validation lessens. They become less dependent on being needed, and they connect more deeply with their own feelings. They still perceive themselves as helpful, but they no longer need to be constantly serving others to prove that they possess inherent self-worth. By releasing this compulsion to please others in order to have value, their pride melts away and they find rest in humility, which creates a much healthier overall self-perception rooted in authenticity and truth.

Type Three

In low awareness, Threes conflate what they do with who they are. They avoid looking within themselves to discover who they truly are and instead live in a fictional story line. Their self-perception is so strongly oriented toward the opinions and approval of others that they automatically morph into whatever role they sense will make them appear successful in the minds of the particular group they are with. Over time, Threes play so many different roles for so many different people that they lose all sense of self underneath the performance. Their fear of reconnecting with their truest nature locks them into a cycle of avoiding their own feelings since they believe feelings will only get in the way of accomplishing the goals they think will make them appear worthy.

In high awareness, Threes slow down and reconnect with their own emotions. They identify what they truly value and rediscover their authentic selves. They pay less attention to how they are being perceived by other people and more attention to what they genuinely value. They do this with less emphasis on tasks and more investment in interpersonal relationships—not just the strategic relationships that make them more successful but also the relationships built solely on love and mutual care. They become much more present to themselves and begin to give themselves permission to have their own unique identity without concern for the expectations of others. They learn to see themselves as worthy for just being who they were created to be, not for what they can accomplish.

Type Four

In low awareness, Fours perceive themselves as fundamentally flawed or different from others. They think of themselves as outsiders, as if they don't really belong to the group. They romanticize people and situations in their minds and feel frustrated that their own circumstances will never meet the ideal they've created. Fours naturally focus on what is missing, including within themselves; their self-perception is skewed toward believing they lack some basic key to happiness that other people come by naturally. This may lead them into cycles of moving toward other people, becoming disillusioned, and then withdrawing in an unconscious confirmation that they don't, in fact, belong.

In high awareness, Fours perceive themselves as wonderfully unique, imaginative, and creative. They see beauty in things that others miss, and they are grounded in the present rather than romanticizing the past or the future. In this truer perception of themselves, they trust the unique role they play in the group and realize that nothing was ever missing. Instead of their differences leading them into isolation, Fours appreciate the gifts they bring and experience belonging.

Type Five

In low awareness, Fives perceive themselves as completely independent, self-sufficient, private, and knowledgeable—all of which are true. However, what they often refuse to see is that these self-perceptions (and corresponding behaviors) are rooted in a fear of incompetence, a disconnection from their emotions, and the false belief that they need to constantly protect themselves and their resources or they will be depleted beyond recovery.

In high awareness, Fives are grounded—connected to their body and feelings. They trust they have enough and that their sense of self isn't really under threat. Their mental preoccupation with information gathering is led by curiosity rather than scarcity, and they connect to their emotions without fear. They still cherish their cerebral prowess, but now they value their entire selves—head, heart, and body.

Type Six

In low awareness, Sixes feel as though they lack guidance or support structures. They perceive themselves as endangered by a frightening world and worry they won't have what it takes to navigate the pits and potholes of life without falling in. Although they are driven by fear, they deny these fears, reframing their behavior as merely being thoughtful, responsible, or prepared. They attach themselves to relationships as a means to feel protected and safe.

In high awareness, Sixes experience what it means to have faith and confidently lead themselves through life's complexities. They acknowledge fear when it arises, without shame, and metabolize their concerns openly and freely before moving forward. They see themselves as the warm, supportive, and loyal friends and colleagues they are.

Type Seven

In low awareness, Sevens perceive themselves as unencumbered adventurers who love excitement and new experiences. In their minds, they are intrepid explorers, constantly craving more in the sense that they want to experience a little bit of all possibilities. They believe in staying positive and feel that it is their role to reframe negatives into positives for themselves and their friends, families, and teams. In organizational settings, they may believe that it's always their job to inspire and motivate their teams toward all they can achieve. What they fail to perceive about themselves, however, is how all of this is rooted in the fear that if they ever slow down and take in the fullness of reality without reframing the hard parts, they will become trapped in pain. Perpetual reframing robs them of the full spectrum of emotions and may prevent them from fully engaging in growth work.

In high awareness, Sevens loosen their grip on the misconception that they need more and begin to appreciate that their daily needs are already being met. This is a mindset shift from striving to trusting. They take pleasure in having limits and experience the value of being still. They are content with less. They become less focused on future possibilities and release the compulsion to point out silver linings or reframe every bad experience as a blessing in disguise. They take life as it comes.

Type Eight

In low awareness, Eights see themselves as passionate protectors of the weak and vulnerable. They view others as more fragile than they are and believe it is their role to act when others won't—or when they perceive the actions of others as ineffective. Eights believe they experience a wide range of emotions, but in this lower level of awareness, what they are really feeling is intensity (the passion of lust) rooted in a physical posture of defense. This passion overshadows all other, more nuanced feelings. They overuse intensity to protect themselves from feeling weak or vulnerable.

In high awareness, Eights may still be protectors of the weak and vulnerable, but they open up to accept their own vulnerabilities without trying to hide them from others. They stop believing "if you want something done right, you have to do it yourself" and make room for the ideas of others. Instead of being on constant guard on behalf of others, they soften their defensive posture and shift toward developing others' capabilities through coaching and mentoring. Eights let go of needing to be chronically doing something (which is a self-distraction technique) and learn to be present, exploring a broader range of emotions.

Type Nine

In **low awareness**, Nines perceive themselves as less important than everyone else. They have a central issue with anger, but they don't recognize anger in themselves. They believe it is their role to create peace and harmony in their relationships, with their teams, and in their businesses, and they do this through overidentifying with others' wants and feelings while undervaluing their own. In their yearning to avoid conflict, Nines are self-forgetting and self-minimizing in order to remain unaffected by life and all of its tensions.

In **high awareness**, Nines become grounded in their bodies and acknowledge their own anger and needs. They perceive themselves as equal to others and become willing to speak up and assert their views without fear of conflict. They become more decisive and can lead or take action appropriately. They are honest and clear about their own desires rather than either denying them or expressing them in stealthy ways, and they start taking the necessary steps to fulfill their own goals. They start to show up to life.

Self-Perception: From Low to High Awareness

To become self-aware is to live out a truer, healthier story. Each person's Ennea-type was formed in response to their childhood environment and their perception of the world. We formed a view of ourselves and others that isn't objectively accurate but was useful at the time. The problem now is what Carl Jung observed about the human condition: "We cannot live the afternoon of life according to the program of life's morning, for what was great in the morning will be little at evening, and what in the morning was true will at evening have become a lie."[2]

The work of developing emotional intelligence starts with an accurate self-perception. Step one is to acknowledge and accept that we do not naturally see things accurately or objectively. In lower awareness, we see ourselves only through the lenses of the stories we tell about ourselves and others and are disconnected from the essence of who we truly are. In higher awareness, we learn that we are infinitely more than the sum of our experiences, and we begin to rediscover our truest selves.

Learning about our Enneagram type isn't the end of our journey but the beginning. It is an invitation to discover ourselves and to reclaim the parts we've long forgotten. Rediscovering these hidden places requires compassionate self-acceptance. Those who strive to grow from a place of shame, guilt, or insecurity quickly fall back into the reactive patterns that keep them stuck in lower levels of awareness. Shame is counterproductive. We must learn to accept and appreciate all of who we are and the stories that built us if we are to then learn how to release those stories in exchange for something better. This is what it means for us to be like the new mother beholding her newborn, filled with wonder, love, and gratitude. And to gaze upon ourselves like the good father does, seeing how remarkable we are. When we can look at ourselves with that kind of attunement and love, we then have the capacity for meaningful change.

I was recently speaking with someone who identifies as a Six on the Enneagram. At some point in our conversation, she mentioned that she was dreading an upcoming social gathering. This group was filled with some contentious individuals, and she already felt fatigued from the work she predicted she would be tasked with doing to keep social dynamics from completely falling apart. I asked her why she felt it was her responsibility to hold things together, and she replied, "Because no one else will." To which I responded with what all brilliant coaches would say is the most important question you can learn in coaching school: "*And . . . ?*" "And I'm afraid of what will happen to these relationships if I don't," she exclaimed.

In other words, she perceived herself as the responsible one in this group and was motivated by the fear of fragmentation among some of the important relationships she depended on to help life feel more predictable and secure, even at the expense of discomfort and fatigue. We went on to explore how this perception was blocking her from being able to relax and have faith that things will work out, and how she will be safe, secure, and still a loyal friend without carrying the burden of trying to hold things together that perhaps aren't meant to be. Up until that moment, her self-perception as the mortar for this house of friends was diverting her attention from her own growth and well-being and causing her to feel stuck in playing a role she no longer wanted to play, resulting in a lot of anxiety. She needed to give herself permission to perceive herself differently, more accurately.

Moving toward higher levels of awareness means letting go of beliefs that are no longer serving us. We cannot change what we do until we change how we see ourselves.

Reflections

1. Pause and take inventory of your physical and emotional needs right now. What sensations are you experiencing? What are your emotions telling you?

2. Regardless of your Ennea-type, take captive any intrusive thoughts or false stories that steal your peace. What is your inner dialogue right now? Is it true? Is it serving you?

3. What are you most proud of? Write it down and pin it up somewhere you'll be able to see it over and over again.

4. What is the kindest thing someone has said about your character? Write it down and place it next to the thing you're most proud of.

4

Self-Expression

There is no greater agony than bearing an untold story inside you.

Maya Angelou

How do you express yourself?

Are you proper and reserved? Do you tend to move toward people with enthusiasm and bravado? Are you searching the room for subtle clues about what is and isn't acceptable in this particular environment? Or do you prefer to withdraw into your interior world and express yourself through reading about relatable characters and journaling your most private emotional experiences?

Maybe none of these descriptions are true of you. Perhaps you prefer to express yourself through power and force of will—"my way or the highway." Or perhaps you haven't really thought about it much, and you tend to just do you according to the mood and circumstances you're in that day.

Each Enneagram type has a natural focus of attention that feeds an automated habit of expression. These habitual self-expression patterns are often part of the denied self. We outsource the reasons for our interpersonal conflicts, failed relationships, and lack of intimacy as an external problem of unfortunate circumstances instead of looking deep within ourselves to evaluate honestly how we might be getting in our own way.

I have a friend who leads with type Five. She carries with her this need to feel competent and self-sufficient because her inaccurate self-perception is that her competency and intellect are the most valuable things about her. The only way to try to feel safe in such a chaotic world is by becoming knowledgeable. Her self-perception feeds her self-expression, which in this case is through a tendency to wall off emotions or anything or anyone who might interfere with her determination to engage the world solely through the mind.

She desires meaningful friendships and has confided in me that she doesn't know why others don't seem to want to engage with her the way she'd like, not recognizing that often when new acquaintances move toward her, she automatically moves away—not physically but up into the recesses of her mind. Her habit of attention and corresponding habit of expression are so programmed that she cannot see how she's being perceived, which leaves her feeling sad and lonely at times. Her self-expression denotes to others that she is observing life instead of living it.

The challenge of becoming aware of our self-defeating tendencies (whatever they may be), and then developing healthy, authentic, balanced self-expression is that all self-expression is inextricably linked to the emotional vice of our core Enneagram type. How we see ourselves, others, and the situations we are in are filtered through this lens. When we are communicating from our personalities, we are sending and receiving messages from our Ennea-type's passion. In other words, our truest selves—the parts of us we freely shared with the world in childhood before we learned that it was unsafe to be that way—are buried beneath the armor and defense mechanisms of personality. And these personas

Type	Habit of Attention (rooted in faulty self-perception)	Habit of Expression
One	Perceives themselves to be corrupt or defective somehow; looks for what's wrong and how they can improve it.	Quickly starts categorizing people and things into boxes of right and wrong; may appear rigid and resentful.
Two	Perceives themselves to be possibly unworthy of love; looks for a particular person to connect with.	Uses flattery and unsolicited help/advice to feel wanted and loved.
Three	Perceives themselves to be somehow lacking in worth; immediately notices the desires, expectations, values, climate, clothing, and overall vibe in every room.	Automatically adapts to become the best representation of that environment.
Four	Perceives themselves to be without significance; immediately feels what is missing by introjecting the aesthetics and metaphors of their surroundings.	Compares the current experience to that of an idealized past experience; may express dissatisfaction with the present.
Five	Perceives that they may be only as useful and safe as the knowledge they procure; assesses who or what in the room may steal the energy they need for their pursuits.	Creates emotional buffers between themselves and others; often appears standoffish or aloof.
Six	Perceives that they are without the necessary support or guidance; scans for all potential hazards and threats.	Overly questions plans and authority in order to feel safe and prepared.
Seven	Perceives that they are at risk of deprivation and pain; scans for all possible opportunities to enhance their experience.	Appears distracted and/or disinterested in anything or anyone who may limit them.
Eight	Perceives that they must protect themselves from being controlled or taken advantage of; scans for who has the power in the room.	Challenges anyone who is deemed to be ineffective with their authority; may also create conflict to surface any possible hidden agendas.
Nine	Perceives themselves to be at risk of being cut off from others; quietly listens for the consensus around the table.	Minimizes their presence and simply merges with opinions of others.

are always being fed by our emotional vice like an IV drip inserted directly in our vein. They wouldn't survive otherwise.

The bad news is that it takes a tremendous amount of mental and emotional energy to try to overcome, or even manage, these personalities of ours. When we are told to be more like someone else or to "take it down a notch," we are forced to pivot our communication style from an already partially inauthentic place and create an even further forged self in order to appease the wishes of the person giving us this feedback. We may succeed for a time until our resources are depleted and we no longer have the energy to maintain the facade. This is why coaching interventions fail so much of the time. Creating meaningful and lasting shifts means we have to begin by recovering what we've lost before we can even consider adding on.

The good news, however, is that we can recover an authentic, healthy, and sustainable expression of self when we are able to observe the egoic place from which we learned to communicate, allow ourselves to become a little disgusted by its insincerity, and then slowly learn to set aside these masks and allow our genuine selves to arrive. This does not negate what I said about self-acceptance in the previous chapter. Only by accepting all of what is true about ourselves, without judgment, can we cultivate the curiosity needed to explore the stories and self-limiting beliefs behind the mask. Self-acceptance seeds the ground for our growth, creating the conditions by which we learn to love ourselves too much to continue living in a story that is no longer serving us. As we begin to move from vice to virtue, the armor we've been wearing no longer feels attractive to us, and we can finally be free to express the totality of who we really are.

Some practical suggestions for how to move from vice to virtue are presented at the end of this chapter. As you read through the ways in which the various types might express themselves, notice the presence of the emotional vice (aka passion) that is present in the low-awareness description and the respective virtue that shows up in the high-awareness description.

Type	Emotional Vice (personality)	Virtue (reclaimed self)
One	Anger	Serenity
Two	Pride	Humility
Three	Self-deception	Authenticity
Four	Envy	Equanimity
Five	Avarice	Nonattachment
Six	Fear	Courage
Seven	Gluttony	Sobriety
Eight	Lust (Intensity)	Innocence
Nine	Sloth	Right action

Enneagram Types and Self-Expression

Type One

In low awareness, Ones hold their anger in due to a belief that anger isn't good. Yet the anger often seeps out as a bubbling resentment toward themselves, others, systems, and institutions that fail to live up to their standards. In lower levels of awareness, Ones don't believe that this resentment is being perceived by others. They convince themselves they are being measured solely on merit and the quality of their contributions, not on their disposition (which they believe is in check and sometimes even turned into an overly sunny personality, complete with big toothy smiles). However, to others they may appear rigid and unwavering as they believe they *know* the right way of doing things.

I know a One who is committed to serving the needs of various marginalized groups in his community. He wakes up every day determined to help solve systemic issues that create unfair, disparate outcomes in the lives of people. His passion for righting the wrongs he sees is an inspiration to all who know him and is a great example of how Body types naturally focus on matters of justice and particularly how Ones desire to improve things. However, sometimes he can become so convinced he *knows* the best way to meet a particular need in his community that he stops listening to what the needs might actually be. In his quest for social justice, he has at times ignored the advice and requests of those closest to the problem. Instead, he invested considerable time and resources into a solution he *knew* would work better than what was being suggested. In his quest to improve the lives of those around him, he can become quite rigid about what to do and how to do it. When his efforts are resisted or redirected by those closest to the issues, his body tenses and his temperature rises. You can see the battle within as he expresses his ongoing convictions while trying hard to keep his growing anger between the navigational buoys.

In high awareness, Ones do less: less scheduling, less striving, less criticizing of themselves and others. They begin to release their grip on self-imposed ideals and the belief that they need to be perfect. They become more comfortable with gray areas and start to see loveliness in subtle imperfections, while still retaining their ethics, as they learn to internalize different points of view and become less rigid about their own ideals. They express a greater openness to experimenting with new ideas and solutions to problems. They continue to offer their gifts of improving but are no longer focused on perfecting. These Ones have come to understand that perfection isn't up to them, and they begin to express a posture of acceptance for what they cannot control.

Type Two

In low awareness, Twos' focus of attention is directed toward a particular person or group to connect with. They sense what someone may need (though this is often a projection of their own, unacknowledged needs) and then use flattery to work their way into a position of being able to offer unsolicited advice. For them, self-expression means unconsciously seeking out opportunities to help others in order to satiate their ego's need to be needed. They will often deny their own feelings and needs and overdo expressions of empathy and service in an attempt to feel worthy of being loved.

In lower levels of awareness, Twos' giving is less altruistic than it is transactional. When their help isn't appropriately appreciated, it isn't uncommon for Twos to express anger and resentment toward the object of their unrequited giving. This is the passion of pride as they are unable to recognize or consider that others may not be dependent on them or want their help.

In high awareness, Twos' attention is more balanced between themselves and others. They are more connected to their own feelings and needs and more direct in communicating them to others. They remain generous, but this generosity becomes truly about the other person and not about getting their own unexpressed needs met. In this way, Twos become more selfless leaders, expressing warmth, empathy, and compassion without any of the entanglements of codependence that can plague this type in lower levels of awareness. In higher awareness, Twos say and do less as they no longer believe they always know the best way to help someone or if their help is even wanted. They are still very much available to help or offer advice when asked, but they are no longer compulsively driven to.

Type Three

In low awareness, Threes constantly gauge what others expect of them and calculate what would make the biggest impact, and then they automatically become the best representation of that expression. Their self-expression is entirely about what they imagine others want them to be. They do this effortlessly, becoming something they aren't over and over again until they have completely lost touch with themselves. They confuse the adapted self for the genuine one, reflecting their emotional vice of self-deception. They are so good at this chameleonlike behavior that they often receive applause and accolades for their performances, which they internalize and mistakenly believe to be a validation of their worth. This leads them to get stuck in a cycle of performing for affirmation when what they want most in the world is to believe they could be considered worthy for just being who they truly are.

In high awareness, Threes embody authenticity. They no longer push aside feelings and instead allow themselves to experience and express the fullness of their emotions. From this higher level of awareness, Threes reclaim the truth that of all Enneagram types, they feel the most! That may come as a surprise to some Threes since they often struggle to access the emotions they have naturally. But at high awareness they begin to move through life with an unapologetic honesty and sincerity and without conforming to anyone's expectations of them. Grounded in the body and in the mind, they slow down, become more present to the people around them, listen more carefully, and start to trust that things will unfold the way they are meant to with or without their involvement. They no longer deceive themselves into believing they are the only ones who can make something happen—that without them everything falls apart—and begin to express a genuine ability to allow others to make decisions, even if the decision isn't the shiniest choice.

Type Four

In low awareness, Fours unconsciously internalize and filter their present circumstances through an idealized version of the past to give meaning to the moment and significance to their own existence. This idealized (and often untrue) memory sets them on a path of perpetual disappointment with the way things actually are and may reinforce chronically low self-esteem about how they interact with the world and how the world interacts with them. They then try to compensate for this internalized lacking by cultivating an idealized image about who they are, which often changes with the tides of their emotional currents. The resulting frustration feeds a habit of attention and self-expression that is hardwired to focus on what is absent. Fours' pain then expresses itself as variations of sorrow and suffering, which can be histrionic and unpredictable.

In high awareness, Fours loosen their grip on the false belief that they are fundamentally flawed or without personal significance. They cease conjuring an idealized image and begin to actually see the tremendously positive qualities and gifts they naturally possess. Their habit of attention begins to look outward without making comparisons as to whether they are better than or less than anyone else. This paves the way for them to notice less of what is missing and more of what is good without losing any of the creativity most Fours bring to the table. At this level of awareness, the focus is on what *is*, which expresses itself as gratitude, appreciation, and consistency.

Type Five

In low awareness, Fives can be self-isolating, resisting the fullness of life. They withhold time and resources from a fear that they will become depleted if those precious commodities aren't defended. This guardedness expresses itself as a continuous inflexibility with others; these Fives seem unwilling to jump in to help the team with a last-minute task or project that was unplanned. Their proclivity to withdraw into their minds as a means for safeguarding their resources often makes others feel that they are unknowable on a personal level; the Five may share information about themselves but doesn't connect on a heart level. These Fives talk about and analyze feelings but do not let themselves *feel* their feelings, especially not in real time.

In high awareness, Fives' hearts are open, and they spring to life! They no longer operate from the self-limiting and untrue belief that they will be depleted by the requests directed at them, both internal and external. Freed of that fear of engulfment, they become willing to give of themselves freely and generously, from both their heads and their hearts. Instead of withholding their resources, they start to live with openhandedness. They also become open to diverse points of view as they release the belief that they must be the one who can best understand any complex problem. They even begin to resist the compulsive desire to break everything down into its component parts and instead can stand back and appreciate the whole.

Type Six

In low awareness, Sixes express ongoing apprehension over what could go wrong in a variety of scenarios. While all Ennea-types experience fear in their own specific ways, Sixes often live from a more generalized anxiety—their fears are more comprehensive. However, in lower levels of awareness, Sixes may not understand their doomsday preparations as being motivated by fear (especially for the One-to-One subtype of Six that is considered counterphobic instead of phobic) but as careful planning. While they can be brilliant verbal processors who think out loud in order to work out all possible perils, in low awareness they may become contrarian for the sake of testing other people's ideas and calculations, even when they are backed by data. While this approach can be helpful at times, it can also quickly move from problem-solving to problem seeking, which is an act of aggression toward the unknown. The ongoing search for certitude is a hallmark of a Six's self-expression in lower levels of awareness.

In high awareness, Sixes stop seeing things as a binary calculation of safe versus unsafe because they become more confident that even in the midst of possibly difficult circumstances, they are secure, courageous, and self-reliant. In realizing this truth, they release their dependence on worry and the lie that they are without support or guidance and can't rely on themselves to be safe or make right decisions. In higher levels of awareness, Sixes no longer strive to become stronger or more courageous, reaching desperately for safety. The safety comes naturally when they simply let go of the delusions and deceptions and return to who they truly are—the manifestation of which expresses itself as courage rooted in conviction.

Type Seven

In low awareness, Sevens express enthusiasm to avoid accepting unpleasant realities and to keep themselves from feeling cornered in the present moment. They deny the fear that's inside of them and frenetically multitask as a means to stay busy and distracted. They want to avoid feeling or expressing sadness at all costs, so they choose a frenzied sort of cheerfulness. In many ways, they perpetually run from their fear of suffering in shoes of optimism. In their desire to reframe negatives into positives, they look only at the data that confirms their views and avoid any evidence that contradicts them.

In high awareness, Sevens stop believing that they need to run after the next big thing in order to feel unfettered. They learn to like what they are doing now instead of perpetually focusing attention on the future. They become free from their own self-limiting desires and are able to move from excessive stimulation, in which they try to do multiple things at once, to a life that is simple and fulfilling. They can see themselves as responsible adults because they understand the need to say no. They are no longer so enthusiastic with themselves and are content with less.

Type Eight

In low awareness, Eights are larger than life—you can feel them walk into a room about a minute before they get there. They immediately scan for who has the power in the room in order to evaluate and possibly challenge that power. In low awareness, Eights express the most anger of any type on the Enneagram. To them, it doesn't feel like anger; it's an overflowing sense of passion.

This passion is felt so intensely (especially where matters of social injustice are concerned) that it can overtake them, making their self-expression bigger and more intense than it may need to be. Eights naturally care for and want to protect the weak and the underdog, but in lower levels of awareness, the emotional vice of lust consumes and conceals all other milder feelings. In that state, Eights' self-expression is all about power, leaving the vulnerable caught in the eye of the storm that is the supremacy of the Eight (the exact opposite of what the Eight wants).

In high awareness, Eights reduce their oppositional energy and no longer automatically scan for who has the power, nor do they compulsively desire to challenge that person. They get in touch with softer, more tender emotions and no longer experience weakness as something to avoid at all costs. Rather, they celebrate it, recognizing that the greatest strength they possess is vulnerability. From this place of vulnerability, they remain committed to justice and fairness but are slower to spring into action. This allows them space to contemplate their choices before making a decision, which leads to more holistic and empathetic outcomes for all involved. Eights in high awareness are able to fully consider and honor multiple and diverse perspectives.

Type Nine

In low awareness, Nines tend to make themselves smaller than they are and avoid expressing their authentic selves. They minimize their own importance and then get stuck in comfortable routines as a tactic to avoid upsetting the apple cart. This hesitation to show up may convey messages of overt agreement with others, even when they do not agree. Nines can become known for a scattered kind of procrastination, failing to follow through on things they said they would do—all because they could not directly say no to tasks they never wanted to do in the first place. This passivity is an unconscious strategy for trying to stay asleep to the anger they fear acknowledging.

In high awareness, Nines express themselves fully. They show up. Instead of simply keeping the peace through sitting on the sidelines or denying their own desires, self-aware Nines are fully self-remembering. They are willing to state their views, even if they are upsetting to someone. They are a force to be reckoned with, intentionally disrupting previous routines and trying things that force them to connect with all of who they are, including their anger. They no longer live life on the surface—they are now in the depths.

Self-Expression: From Low to High Awareness

Our self-expression is intimately linked to our self-perception. What we believe informs much of what we feel, which then influences our actions. All of this is in constant motion inside of us, happening on a mostly unconscious level. Our beliefs are largely composed of what we've experienced in the past and what we are predicting about the future. The very things we see and do are all routed through beliefs about ourselves, others, and the world around us. Our brains create emotional states within us based on the physical well-being of our bodies in any given moment while also incorporating data from our past experiences (whether or not those experiences are fully understood) and what they predict is about to happen based on sensory input from all around us.[1]

Left to our own devices, we simply react to stimuli. Something happens and we react. And our reactions often happen faster than our conscious thoughts can process. The doctor taps our knee and the leg kicks. It isn't our will or choice; it's just reactivity. What working with a psycho-spiritual, sense-making system like the Enneagram helps us to do is open up the space between stimulus and response. It creates distance between something happening and our responding to it. And over time, it reveals to us all the ways we react that are limiting or self-defeating. It unlocks in us the choice to express ourselves differently. By removing reactivity, we reclaim our agency.

A friend of mine once shared a story about someone she knew and cared for who identified as a type Four. In his early adulthood, this young man became known as an emotionally volatile, almost unstable individual. His self-perception at the time was that he was a very damaged person who had been through a tragic childhood. However, when confronted with examples of people who had experienced even more tragic childhoods, his tragedy just didn't ring true in his social circle. His identity—the story he was telling himself about himself and about the world—was designed to emphasize the very saddest things that had happened in his life, such as losing a grandparent.

Of course, other people only saw the way he expressed himself and not his underlying fears, doubts, or desires, which led him to covet a deeply meaningful life with strong connections. He exaggerated his own misfortunes and seemed incapable of giving a genuine sense of attention to other people's challenges. Others kept him at arm's length because he was so unpredictable—one day idolizing a friend or romantic partner and the next day wanting nothing to do with them. All this stemmed from his untrue belief that he was defective.

Once he committed to doing personal growth work, his self-perception began to change, and he was able to accept himself as complete. He no longer engaged in these bids for other people's sympathies. His self-expressions changed because his self-perception became clearer, and he was able to break the cycle of reactivity that was keeping him locked into a narrative that was working against everything he wanted for his life but didn't believe he deserved. From a place of healing and wholeness, he learned to develop and enjoy more fulfilling friendships.

To help us widen that space between stimulus and response, we need to understand that there are no good or bad emotions. There are just emotions. There are, of course, positively and negatively *experienced* emotions. All emotions are data, and the negatively experienced emotions often hold the most important data of all.

They point to where a core need or expectation isn't being met and can also illuminate where our Ennea-type's emotional vice is harming us.

Each feeling is pointing us toward an important truth that requires our attention. Whether an emotion is pleasant or unpleasant, there are, of course, healthy and unhealthy *expressions* of these emotional states and feelings. As we saw in the previous chapter, the first building block of healthy self-expression is to become grounded in a healthy and true self-perception. And the truest self-perception we can embrace is that we are so much more than our personalities. Our personalities are the waterline, but the essence of who we are is the deep water running below what is visible on the surface. Our personalities are part of who we are, but they certainly aren't *all* of who we are. When we truly come to understand this, our beliefs about ourselves begin to shift, and we reconnect to the whole of who we are—a more complete and integrated self led by our deepest values and true desires. From integration and wholeness, then, our behaviors and expressions become aligned and consistent with our virtues.

You can take an important step toward building higher awareness by telling trusted others your story—your *real* story. Above all else, growing our capability for healthy self-expression means sharing our truth with others—letting the trusted people in our lives into our experiences and the self-limiting beliefs we carry that hold us back. Once we get honest with ourselves and begin to reconnect to our authenticity, we must show it to the world, otherwise it isn't authentic. Healing and wholeness are found in freeing our stories with confident, openhanded sharing through confessing the masks we are inclined to wear and asking our community to help us finally live without them.

Reflections

Think of a time when you reacted to something and lived to regret it. Once you've identified it, answer (and actually write down your answers!) the following questions:

1. What were you feeling at the time?
2. What was the story you were telling yourself about the other person/circumstance?
3. What story were you believing about yourself at the time?
4. What were the consequences of your reaction?

Now let's try a reframing exercise:

1. What feelings were you excluding from your own conscious awareness at the time of your reaction?
2. What's an alternative story that might have been true about the other person/circumstance at the time?
3. In what ways was the story you were believing about yourself limiting or exaggerated?
4. Given the alternatives you've just identified, how could you have responded differently? What might the outcome have been if you had?

5

Interpersonal Relationships

We are like islands in the sea, separate on the surface but connected in the deep.

William James

Who matters most to you? What is the role of relationships in your life? What kind of friend are you? What kind of colleague? How would others describe your leadership? And what would your closest family members say about you?

I don't always like considering the answers to these questions. I'd much rather assume the best about myself and the worst about those who disagree with me. The heart is well-defended territory and prefers us to be less than completely honest with it. So when confronting painful questions about ourselves, we may let the head rationalize and the body protect what the heart can't bear to feel.

The problem with that strategy, of course, is that we remain willfully ignorant, hidden from ourselves and others. And it's not just the unpleasant realities that get hidden in the process; we inevitably hide away some of the most beautiful parts as well. We are not so clever as to deny only unpleasant realities, for each one of those is rooted in and connected to important truths about who we are. When those truths get locked away, our relationships can begin to feel a bit shallow and unsatisfying because we aren't fully present in them—only our well-crafted, well-defended personas are. And others aren't experiencing the fullness of who we are. Intimacy is swallowed up in our ego's demand that we carefully curate and present an image of whatever our particular Enneatype most values: we want to be seen as good, likable, admirable, special, knowledgeable, careful, fun, strong, or amiable, so that's what we present.

Until we do the hard work of waking up, we are living at a distance from ourselves and others, unsure where our image ends and we begin. However, when we begin to recover the depths of our truest selves, we can learn to perceive how we are seeing, understand what we are feeling, and observe what we are thinking. We've already laid the groundwork for emotional intelligence by digging into our self-perception and our self-expression, so we have a stable foundation. As I stated earlier, cultivating these first two EQ skills can help us widen the space between stimulus and response, enabling us to be more genuine and intentional. And that leads us to a third skill: when we become more genuine with ourselves and others—when we better understand who we are beyond the persona we've been offering the world—we can engage in deep, fulfilling interpersonal relationships.

Life is fundamentally about relationships. How we relate to our partners and children, how teams interact, and how customers are served all depend upon the health of our interpersonal relationships. When someone quits, a business deal goes bad, or someone swears to never do business with so-and-so again, these are often principally influenced by at least one dissatisfying or upsetting interpersonal experience.

We crave and depend on healthy relationships to feel connected, satisfied, hopeful, and cared for. And yet, cultivating healthy, long-lasting relationships is one of life's greatest challenges. If you're anything like me, you've lost touch with many of the people you once couldn't have imagined doing life without. And if you're like me, you've had your heart broken and you've broken some-one else's. You have regrets about how you handled an important conversation with someone or how you didn't show up for a friend in need the way you could have . . . the way you should have. Even self-aware individuals can struggle with the complexity of devel-oping and maintaining important and satisfying relationships.

Returning to the Intelligence Centers

Healthy interpersonal interactions require, at minimum, two people who are self-aware and sensitive to the needs and wants of the other. But within the confines of every intimate encounter, we each tend toward a particular engagement style. We are always moving either toward, away from, or against the people in our lives. The three Enneagram intelligence centers—Body, Heart, and Head—help to reveal which one of these approaches we tend to take. As we saw in chapter 1, each intelligence center has a default setting. And the Ennea-types within a particular intelligence center share a com-mon posture toward how they're inclined to approach interpersonal relationships as part of each type's unconscious strategy to feel safe and get their respective needs met. Let's take another look at these groupings before exploring relationships in low and high awareness.

Body Types

The default tendency for Body types (Eight, Nine, and One) is to move *against* others. Although these three Enneagram types seem quite different from one another, they all share a central issue with anger. The anger is there, in part, as a refusal to accept reality. Knowing that things are broken, they adopt a posture of standing against things the way they are. This is why Body types share a central conviction to right injustices and advocate for social reform. However, because they instinctively believe they know the right and wrong ways of approaching a problem, they are unlikely to allow other people to impose ideas upon them that are contrary in any way to the convictions they hold in their gut. Eights may run over you, Nines may passively nod an implied agreement with you, and Ones may refrain from argument because it isn't considered good, but all three types in their own way move against others to protect their own convictions. They may not succeed in forcing their will upon you, but they will resist allowing your will to be forced upon them.

Because of their instinctual *knowing* how something is supposed to be, they tend toward rigidity and may struggle to see shades of gray (particularly true of Ones and Eights). Body types often lack nuance as they prefer things to be more concrete. This is a central part of their dominant experience with anger, which in relationship is often experienced by others as intensity from Eights, passive-aggressive stubbornness from Nines, and resentment from Ones.

If you are in a personal or professional relationship with a Body type, it is helpful to remember that they have an internal compass that guides them. They get into action more quickly than the other types (though the action that Nines get into is often not in their own best interest). Body types often swing into motion while Head types are still contemplating and Heart types are processing emotions.

Body types are hands-on. When working with them, be willing to be spontaneous. Listen to their instincts and connect to their sense of fairness and justice. Instead of using thinking or feeling language with them, try asking for their *impressions* and *perceptions*, which is the language of instincts and the senses.

Heart Types

The default tendency for Heart types (Two, Three, and Four) is to move *toward* others. As we looked at earlier, each Heart type shares a central issue with sadness. This sadness, in part, is rooted in the experience of feeling separated from the essence of who they are. More than Head and Body types, Heart types intuit what it is like to wear the mask of personality, and they mourn the distance between the mask and the real person beneath it. This is not to say that Heart types go through life feeling sad all the time, but there is a sense of dejection from the experience of being detached from authenticity and, therefore, not valued by others for who they *really* are.

Of course, the ways that Twos, Threes, and Fours deal with this dissonance vary greatly. Twos who struggle to connect to their own feelings and sense of identity will rely on the affirmation of others in order to feel wanted. They move toward others to befriend and please as a strategy for resolving emotional dissonance through receiving affirmation for their efforts. Threes move toward others to understand the desires and expectations of others in order to meet and exceed those expectations and perform for approval. Fours move toward others to compare themselves and their experiences to see whose story is better or worse. After they've been in close enough proximity to make a comparison, they may then withdraw themselves to process resulting emotions. But when they do, they hope the other person will pursue them.

Despite these differences in how the Heart types go about getting the love they need, all three naturally move toward others for validation and approval. Therefore, Heart types can be good at supporting others as their energies are automatically attuned to the emotional experiences around them. However, because they are trying to resolve the sadness of their own experience, this empathetic expression is often motivated by an unconscious desire for others to mirror back validation.

Since this is a chapter on relationships and the Heart types are all about relationships, you may be thinking that the Heart types have an innate advantage in this aspect of emotional intelligence. And in one sense they do: their keen ability to use their heart to read the world and the people they encounter is an inborn gift of emotional intelligence. However, their need to feel valued by others can stunt their ability to develop a healthy grounding, leading to some possible neuroses: Do you like me or not? Should I feel good about myself or not? Their insecurities can undermine the quality of their relationships.

If you are in a personal or professional relationship with a Heart type, it is helpful to remember that they prefer to take in information through *feeling language* and are more concerned with how they are being perceived and received than the other types. If you've ever heard of the concept of a "feedback sandwich," it was likely from a Heart type. This feedback model starts with an expressed appreciation for a person, is followed by addressing a behavior you'd like to see changed, and ends with supportive language to help enable the desired change and reaffirm your appreciation. Now, there is some debate as to the efficacy of this model, but the point here is simply this: Heart types are exponentially more concerned with how others feel about them than the other types.

I worked with someone who identified as a type Three who told me often that they liked receiving feedback about their work. However, I quickly observed that their first reaction to critiques was often emotionally charged defensiveness. It became evident to me that when they told me they desired frequent feedback, what they were really asking was to know how I felt about them.So I adopted the feedback sandwich model, and it did wonders for our relationship, their confidence, and their progress. This is the language of Heart types. Please don't try this with an Eight.

Head Types

The default tendency for Head types (Five, Six, and Seven) is to move *away* from others, which they do to overcorrect for their fear. Fives withdraw from others because they fear being overwhelmed. Sevens, who are afraid of being trapped, move away from others to pursue a future they think will be free of restrictions or limitations. And Sixes . . . well, Sixes are something of an anomaly. Sixes could be said to move toward others in that they are the Loyalists of the Enneagram, and when it comes to their inner circle, they tend to be fiercely committed (though in low awareness this is more transactional as a strategy to feel secure). Or they could be seen as moving against others at times as they are the most contrarian of all types, ready to challenge and question all ideas others share, sometimes to the detriment of long-term relational health. However, when considering their general approach to interpersonal relationships, they have a proclivity to move *away*—away into their mind—and constantly question everything, including your loyalty to them. In this way, they remain at a distance from others. Believing their sense of security can be reclaimed through analysis and making sense of things, all three Head types naturally move *away* from others to analyze, question, and plan.

Each Head type tends to waste a lot of energy with overthinking. What this may look like in relationships is that they get caught up in mental entanglements with scenario making, playing out in their minds the different obstacles and problems that could arise. Right below the surface of this catastrophizing is a fear that arises out of being unable to feel secure in an uncertain world. We all feel that, but Head types experience more fear over what they cannot predict than other types tend to, so they try to resolve this with excessive thinking and planning.

This overthinking may present challenges for Heart and Body types who are in relationship with Fives, Sixes, and Sevens. Loved ones may feel that Head types are not really present with them in the moment but rather are somewhere up in their minds, far away in planning or analysis.

If you are in a personal or professional relationship with a Head type, it is helpful to remember that they seek to relate to the world through *logic* and *understanding*. They want to make sense of things and be able to draw concrete conclusions. Hold space for them to do that.

Before we explore low and high awareness in interpersonal relationships for each of the nine core Enneagram types, consider your natural propensity of moving either toward, away, or against others and how the unconscious defense mechanism of your type (see below) shows up in your relationships.

Type	Intelligence Center	Default Relational Tendency	Unconscious Defense Mechanism
One	Body	Move *against*	Reaction formation
Two	Heart	Move *toward*	Repression
Three	Heart	Move *toward*	Identification
Four	Heart	Move *toward*	Introjection
Five	Head	Move *away*	Isolation
Six	Head	Move *away*	Projection
Seven	Head	Move *away*	Rationalization
Eight	Body	Move *against*	Denial
Nine	Body	Move *against*	Narcotization

Enneagram Types and Interpersonal Relationships

Type One

In low awareness, Ones act properly but not genuinely. They work hard to be appropriate in all situations and relationships, though they don't believe they ever quite measure up. (Ones also tend to assume that those around them have the same high expectations, which is often not the case and can lead to problems in relationships.) Their high commitment to a sense of duty in their lives, combined with a strong instinctual belief that they know the difference between right and wrong in almost all circumstances, can contribute to their tendency to move *against* anyone or anything that differs from what their internal compass is telling them. However, Ones try to hide this posture behind the defense mechanism of *reaction formation*—the unconscious strategy of feeling one thing but expressing the opposite in order to be good. This is particularly true of anger, which Ones actively attempt to suppress.

In relationships, they may turn any inward anger they experience into a disingenuous smile through pursed lips because they consider the outward expression of anger to be an inappropriate behavior. Others often perceive Ones as rigid and judgmental, suppressed, and irritated. This perception can make some hesitate to engage freely in relationship with them for fear of criticism. They may worry that they cannot freely reveal their messy and broken parts to Ones and still be accepted and valued by them.

In high awareness, Ones become more present in their relationships, breaking free from the self-defeating cycles of evaluating themselves and others at any given moment. All emotions, including anger, become accepted as valid and sometimes perfectly appropriate. When Ones fully internalize this new understanding, they can properly channel and express any anger they experience. The unexpected outcome is that this freedom produces a calmness and acceptance of themselves and others that Ones never experienced when they were chasing after serenity by trying to perfect the people, places, and things around them.

With dutifulness no longer weighing so heavily on their shoulders, relationships become more honest, transparent, and real. Interpersonal intimacy is now possible as Ones learn to love and reveal their beautifully flawed selves in all of their wonderful messiness.

Type Two

In low awareness, Twos fall quickly into patterns of people-pleasing. They use the defense mechanism of *repression*—the unconscious strategy of suppressing their own internal experience—and redirect their attention outward in search of other people's approval. In this way, they tend to seduce individuals or groups as a strategy for getting others to like them without having to ask anyone directly for anything. This pattern of unconscious seduction enables Twos to manipulate others into helping them feel loved without risking refusal.

Less aware Twos use their feelings to assess what certain others may need and then move *toward* them to meet those needs. Sometimes called the Helper, Twos may use helping as one way to try to please the other person, but that is not the only way in which they please and seduce. Whatever the ploy, it is important to understand that for unaware Twos, everything they do is an unconscious tactic for feeling both loved and protected at the same time. These Twos are desperate for intimacy and at the same time petrified of it because *true* intimacy necessitates that they be in touch with their own feelings and needs and vocalize them clearly in their interpersonal relationships. This is far too risky a proposition for Twos who haven't done their inner work.

In high awareness, Twos' relationships become more authentic and mutual. Twos begin to understand that there is a higher will at work in the universe, so they no longer need to fear that their needs won't be met if they don't compulsively please others. They begin to live and let live, resisting the old patterns of pride and flattery. They no longer believe they are the only ones capable of helping people in the right way. They loosen their grip on needing to constantly stand between a person in need and the task that needs doing. In other words, they begin to feel in their hearts that they themselves may not have any idea what someone truly needs. However, in this higher level of awareness, they remain ready to help when they are invited into a particular story or situation. They make this available to all, as opposed to reserving it for select individuals. Others view them as a gifted resource, but not at all intrusive. When Twos are in this higher level of awareness, their interpersonal skills evolve so that they are no longer impulsively trying to stop everyone's suffering (which is playing God, the passion of pride). Rather, they become loyal friends and colleagues who can sit quietly with those who are suffering.

Type Three

In low awareness, Threes treat relationships as strategic resources for goal achievement. Similar to unaware Twos or Sevens, Threes have their own way of seducing targeted individuals. However, where Twos seduce in order to feel needed and loved, and Sevens seduce through a problem-free, cheerful demeanor to serve their own passion for gluttony,[1] Threes use charm, confidence, and lavish praise to move *toward* others and enlist their help with achieving various aspirations and goals.

Often this is happening on a semiconscious level without any malice intended. But as we've looked at earlier, Threes will simply, and automatically, focus their attention on the desires, expectations, climate, clothing, and overall vibe of any group they are in and then unthinkingly transform themselves into the best representation of whatever that group values. They use the defense mechanism of *identification*—becoming so immersed in the role they are playing that they forget who they really are.

This automatic defense mechanism leads to perpetual self-deception. In relationships, Threes will exchange connecting with you for charming you. In this lower level of awareness, they may appear Seven-ish as their attention wanders from one interesting person to another. However, unlike type Seven, Threes aren't scanning for fun distractions to satiate gluttony but rather are searching for the most important people to impress in order to feed their appetite for worthiness.

There is an old joke about a man who had been going on and on to a woman he was trying to impress—boasting about his money, his trips, his accomplishments, and his connections. He finally takes a breath and says, "But enough about me. Let's talk about you. What do *you* like about *me*?" This is what it can feel like to be in a relationship with a Three until they've done their work and raised their awareness. They're eager, even desperate, for other people's admiration.

If those in positions of power and influence admire them, they believe they will finally feel worthy. In this way, their friends may have felt relationally important to them one minute and dismissed the next, should someone of greater perceived importance enter the Three's field of vision. All of this externally directed energy is the Three's unconscious attempt to avoid their own emotional experience in relationships, settling instead for image validation.

In high awareness, as Threes slow down and learn to be present to themselves and others, their relationships start to become truly interpersonal. Threes can acknowledge and access the personal feelings that they naturally repress, which allows for them to not only "read a room," but to know and "read" themselves. From this authentic place, they are then able to connect with others on a heart level without unconsciously assessing the value the other person may have in service to their agenda.

From this higher level of awareness, Threes stop looking to others to validate their own personal worth. They may even become disgusted by their own vanity as they recognize how their ego fixation has prevented them from experiencing their deepest desire—to know that they could be loved for just being themselves, without any effort or pretense. They now have the courage to be themselves and only themselves which, somewhat ironically, can lead them to receive more admiration than they had before. Now they are admired for their veracity, depth, and relational sincerity instead of their trophy collection.

Type Four

In low awareness, Fours' focus of attention can immediately drift to what feels missing in any relationship. They use the defense mechanism of *introjection*—an unconscious move *toward* others to adopt and internalize the emotions in the room into their own sense of identity. As Enneagram teacher Peter O'Hanrahan describes, "Fours use introjection to avoid ordinariness and maintain a self-image of being authentic. Positive introjection is an attempt to overcome the feeling of deficiency by seeking value from an idealized experience, work or relationship and internalizing this through the emotional center. This also leads to negative introjection: Fours tend to blame themselves for whatever goes wrong in personal relationships."[2] When they walk into a room, they unconsciously project their idealized version of what should be into that room. In this way, Fours are constantly busy with comparisons—of the experiences, places, and people with whom they're engaging.

These comparisons are never objectively accurate as they are rooted deep in the emotional vice of envy. And envy is a liar. It takes captive the Four's tender heart and forces them to constantly evaluate whether they are better or worse than every other person they encounter. There is, of course, no one who is better or worse—we are all created equal. But envy doesn't want Fours to believe that. Instead, it takes hold of their fear of personal deficiency—the false belief that they are fatally flawed somehow—and whispers, "If you can find enough people who aren't as good as you, and if you can find reasons to reject the ones you think might be, then you'll finally feel good enough."

This causes perpetual turmoil for Fours who haven't done their work. They greatly desire deep, authentic emotional connection with people, yet this emotional vice brings about the exact opposite outcome. The further away this takes them from interpersonal intimacy, the more the defense mechanism of introjection comes into play. When they feel emotionally inhibited by another or that the other person is being inauthentic or not making them feel important, this can lead to big emotional expressions in the forms of withdrawal, sadness, and anger.

In high awareness, Fours find equilibrium in their relationships as their emotions are allowed to come and go freely without holding on to any particular feeling for too long. They become less preoccupied with their own inner experience and more genuinely focused on the other person without introjecting what isn't theirs. When they understand that they are more than enough just as they are and that nothing is missing or deficient in them, all comparisons melt away. Grounded in being beautifully authentic and ordinary individuals who fully belong, Fours find a new depth in relationships. This enhanced connection and freedom from conditioned sadness is what Fours have desired all along but could never find by chasing big emotional experiences born from an overidentification with suffering. It is by releasing their grip on deficiency that Fours find abundance.

From this higher level of awareness, Fours become truly present in their relationships and cease to romanticize past experiences and future ideals. They are simply in the here and now, accepting reality as it is. They can find importance and beauty in the simplest experiences while still maintaining their depth. When the tides of life inevitably shift and difficult circumstances arise, aware Fours remain steady and dependable, feeling what they feel but never overidentifying with any one emotion. Instead, emotions become understood and experienced for what they are—an invaluable source of information rather than a source of personal identity.

Type Five

In low awareness, Fives often approach relationships in terms of how other people may add or steal energy away from them. They use the defense mechanism of *isolation*—an emotional and physical move *away* from any situation that feels threatening or overwhelming. It's important to underscore that this moving away isn't conscious, nor is it intended to communicate any offensive message to the other person. At their core, Fives believe they have a finite amount of time and energy to expend each day, so they position themselves to spend these limited resources wisely for fear that they will otherwise become engulfed by an approaching destitution.

Fives are often very sensitive people; it is almost like having sensitive teeth and eating really cold ice cream. This sensitivity leads them to fear feeling too much, so they retreat into the refuge of their minds and process emotions from a safe distance. In relationships, this can cause others to experience the low-aware Five as emotionally unavailable, aloof, uninterested, or even judgmental of other people's emotional experiences and expressions. Fives who have not done the work of becoming aware may struggle to develop interpersonal relationships to the level they reportedly desire because their own emotional self-restraint is incompatible with the emotional vulnerability necessary for connection.

In high awareness, Fives move from observing others to actively engaging with them. These Fives exhibit this inner transformation in their outward behavior, physically stepping into previously unknown spaces or groups with a posture of openness and receptivity. They move beyond themselves and begin to share their knowledge with others because they understand that there is no shortage of knowledge and therefore no need to hoard information. They also no longer need to be the one who knows the most, finding a sense of self beyond their particular area of expertise.

They start listening more actively to all types, not just those whom they've endowed with superior knowledge or insights. They understand that wisdom sits outside of themselves and may come from anywhere. They are no longer attached to knowledge as a mechanism for safety. Their egos soften, their hearts open, and they begin to step into feelings and even start using feeling words in real time when interacting with others.

From this higher level of awareness, Fives discover rewarding and sustainable interpersonal interactions that begin to fuel them rather than diminish their energy. They move from stinginess to abundance, from a heart that closes easily to one that remains open. This only happens when they have grown courageous enough to become vulnerable without fear of the intensity that comes from true intimacy.

Type Six

In low awareness, Sixes may be known and seen as the Loyalists of the Enneagram, which is true, but much of the time these loyalties are unconsciously motivated by a desire to experience security through relationships, rules, or authority figures. Not feeling able to fully trust themselves, they trade away their power to these other relationships and resources as a proactive measure to avert any possible attacks and to avoid facing the inner turmoil of uncertainty.

Sixes fear being without support or guidance, which can lead to expressions of anxiety and defensiveness in relationships. In fact, they typically go to the defense mechanism of *projection*—the unconscious strategy of attributing to others what they cannot accept in themselves. From this place of reactivity, unaware Sixes may frenetically ask more questions or get angry when fear arises. However, they may also become uncharacteristically calm and quiet when something bad actually happens. All these reactions can be difficult to understand by the non-Sixes in their lives.

As stated earlier in this chapter, this type is something of an anomaly in that they seem to move *toward* people and processes that may make them feel safe, move *against* those who may make them feel unsafe by playing the role of contrarian, and move *away* from a true experience of intimacy by always being cerebral and seeking ways to mitigate their fear. I think all these things can be true at point Six on the Enneagram—it represents the panic every type has experienced on some level for having lost connection with their true selves. However, strictly from an interpersonal relationship perspective, I think it is most accurate to say that type Six has the habit of moving *away* from true emotional connection until they are able to open their heart center and step into the courage that true intimacy requires. As long as they are preoccupied with worst-case-scenario planning, they aren't truly available for authentic, vulnerable connection and intimacy.

In high awareness, Sixes relax and begin to trust themselves and their relationships without feeling the need to test others first. As fear gives way to faith, they begin to take full responsibility for themselves and their own lives. They live openly and actively. They begin to assert themselves in healthier ways as cowardice dissipates and is replaced with courage. This includes a broader receptivity to an expanded, more diverse network of people.

From this higher level of awareness, Sixes break free from worst-case-scenario thought loops that have previously threatened to upend the important relationships they most want to protect. They surrender their attempts at controlling all the dangerous outcomes that are possible, recognizing instead that while life is unpredictable, they are strong and capable of meeting any challenges. Life is now. Relationships are now.

Type Seven

In low awareness, the Seven's optimistic, enthusiastic, fun-loving demeanor may make it particularly difficult for others to see the truth. But the more exuberant the Seven's display, the more guarded they are. From this lower level of awareness, Sevens use cheerfulness to beguile others into helping them live life in the clouds, enabling them to avoid unpleasant realities and painful emotions.

While relationships with Sevens can be fun and exciting, they can also be challenging because of the natural resistance they have to slowing down, accepting difficult circumstances for what they are, and being fully present. They use the defense mechanism of *rationalization* to explain away undesirable feelings and to comfort themselves and others. Instead of processing unpleasant situations, they minimize, reframe, or just ignore the negative in order to keep moving. It is their way of staying up in their heads and justifying their behaviors, so they can live at a distance from unwanted emotions and responsibilities.

Because the Seven's default strategy is to avoid limitations, negative data, and uncomfortable emotions, others may perceive them as a bit one-dimensional at times and unavailable—as if they may not take important things seriously enough. When serious circumstances arise, they are likely to move *away* from others to explore stimulating new ideas or undertakings that promise to distract them from unwanted experiences. For Sevens in low awareness, important relational commitments may be sustainable only if they are the ones to initiate the commitment.

In high awareness, Sevens become deeply satisfied with a slower pace, focusing on the person in front of them in the moment without as much pull toward distraction. They allow for more seriousness in their lives and are able to become more committed to people and responsibilities. From this higher level of awareness, Sevens move from imagination to reality, content to be still and appreciate what they already have and where they are. They begin to open themselves up to a fuller spectrum of emotional experience, and intimacy becomes deeper and much more satisfying. They exchange momentary happiness for depth of meaning, accepting that all feelings are essential to experiencing the fullness of life and love—even, perhaps especially, the painful ones.

Type Eight

In low awareness, Eights' interpersonal relationships can be transactional, similar to Twos and Threes. One of my emotional intelligence coaching clients who identifies as an Eight told me, "If it doesn't lead to action, then intimacy is wasted." I couldn't help but laugh when he said this because it so perfectly summarizes the posture of so many Eights, who demand to know, "What is the point of vulnerability?" Eights use the defense mechanism of *denial*—a conscious or unconscious disowning of vulnerability through powering-up energy and intensity—to move *against* people and keep everyone at a safe emotional distance in order to remain in control of their own experience.

Less aware Eights tend to resist intimacy in relationships because intimacy requires vulnerability. Such vulnerability underpins the Eight's primary fear of being controlled or harmed in some way, making intimacy too risky and therefore pointless to them. So they rely on their ability to take charge and be the leader in the vast majority of their relationships. They don't necessarily want to take the lead, but they also won't follow anyone they don't believe is completely right and completely trustworthy. Eights in lower levels of awareness can be oblivious to ways in which their direct, unfiltered demeanor may have hurt or offended other people. In relationships, they can be the proverbial bull in a china shop, causing untold damage because they don't know their own strength. Because they are concerned with fairness as a general rule, it simply doesn't occur to them that the strength they exude over others may not always be fair.

In high awareness, Eights soften and relax more. They release the need to be strong and move quickly all the time. They begin to experience relationships on a more even footing, focusing less on competencies and more on community. They allow their hearts to become exposed and are able to connect with others in an intimate way.

From this higher level of awareness, they're able to offer more empathy to anyone who needs it for they no longer feel the compulsion to act before truly listening. These Eights are comfortable with discomfort and are capable of sitting in and with emotions.

Paradoxically, when they stop trying to be strong, their relation-ships become much stronger. They've discovered their greatest relationship strength is found in what they've spent most of their lives trying to avoid—vulnerability.

Type Nine

In low awareness, Nines are supportive of others but neglectful of themselves. They desire to keep a sense of internal and external peace, so they tend to gravitate toward protecting the status quo and resisting change. They use the defense mechanism of *narco-tization*—a strategy for unconsciously numbing themselves—to avoid anything that feels too big or might wake up the anger they fell asleep to long ago. They actively self-forget through inaction, engaging only in routines and activities that are familiar and re-quire very little mental energy.

Nines who are stuck in this lower level of awareness come across to others as thoughtful, considerate, and easygoing. However, this impression is fueled primarily by a desire to maintain an internal calm and avoid getting in touch with their own desires and feel-ings. As we looked at earlier, while Nines are often referred to as the Peacemakers of the Enneagram, they aren't truly that until they've done the difficult work of waking up to their own inner experience and asserting their will in the world. Until then, they are acting more as peace*keepers*, which is avoidant but not active. After all, avoiding conflict *is* conflict. It's just a passive type of conflict. And passivity is their default strategy for moving *against* others through stubborn resistance.

In high awareness, Nines show up more fully and authentically in their relationships. They become self-remembering and are willing to connect to and express their own opinions and desires without first feeling the need to build consensus or seek approval. They've learned to directly say no when they disagree or don't want to do something.

These Nines no longer fear healthy conflict in their relationships because they no longer believe that conflict will lead to permanent separation from the important people in their lives. They've felt their own anger and now know they are a big and strong enough container to handle it. Like Sevens and Eights who've learned to sit with uncomfortable emotion, knowing it will pass, Nines who've done the hard work of waking up understand that interpersonal conflict can benefit relationships in the long run. After all, iron sharpens iron, but only with a bit of friction.

Interpersonal Relationships: From Low to High Awareness

If our overall happiness and success are indistinguishably linked to the quality of our interpersonal relationships, then why aren't we naturally better at them? While there are many reasons relationships can be difficult to form and maintain, from an Enneagram perspective, the one reason we will focus on for why our professional and personal relationships break down is because we spend most of our lives on autopilot (low awareness). What's more, I think it's likely that we've gone to sleep to each other just as we have to ourselves. After all, how could we possibly be present to someone else if we are asleep to ourselves? How could a life on autopilot ever produce intimacy?

There is no awareness of others without awareness of self, and there is no awareness of self without awareness of others. When all is said and done, growing our emotional intelligence in life, business, leadership, and interpersonal relationships hinges on one thing: *waking up.* Our relationships will thrive or decay in proportion to how awake or asleep we are. When we are living on autopilot, we sometimes treat relationships as merely part of our strategy for trying to get through the day. And when a relationship is no longer helpful in that endeavor, we feel unsatisfied, bored, or disinterested in maintaining it. We often project these feelings onto the other person and begin looking for confirmation that they are the problem instead of us. If it's a professional relationship, we may project our unhappiness onto a performance issue. (Of course, I'm not speaking of times when there really is a breach of trust or performance on the other person's part, but often our opinions are more of a reflection of what is going on with us.) If it's a personal relationship, we may find something about the other that irritates us (which is often something we don't like in ourselves that we see in another) and then pull at that thread until it starts to unravel.

However, when we confront this egoic reality in ourselves, we can begin to see others more clearly and without an agenda. From this place, each of the nine core Enneagram types begins to see everyone as worthy of our best, not because they are useful to us but because we now understand that we are all connected. As Thomas Merton wrote, "Love is our true destiny. We do not find the meaning of life by ourselves alone—we find it with another."[3]

When I first identified my type on the Enneagram, I discovered a mountain of difficult-to-face relationship patterns in my life. It would've been easier to look away, but the Enneagram so accurately described how I'd been showing up to my life—the good, the bad, the ugly—that I felt I was at a crossroads. Either I could continue on the same path and ignore all that the Enneagram was surfacing for me, or I could walk a new path—one that would demand a much slower pace and more stops for proper reflection and would require that I walk alongside others who were choosing to also walk the path.

As a person who leads with type Three, I tend to avoid feeling my own feelings. I've had to reconcile with the ways in which my withholding of emotional expression and my resistance to receiving emotions from others had kept me at arm's length from intimacy in my life. I've had to acknowledge and reflect upon times when I wasn't the type of leader my team needed because I was too focused on putting points on the board instead of really listening to and knowing the people in my care. And I had to get underneath the reasons for this and tend to the wounds of the child within that led to the beliefs that caused some of my relationships to suffer. I had to reconnect with the sadness I'd spent most of my adult life up to that point defending against. And I've had to keep doing that ever since. There are no shortcuts to doing our inner work, and it isn't an item on a to-do list. It's hard work. But when you walk with others who are also committed to their own growth, healing, and wholeness, you find the inspiration to keep going, even on the toughest days.

Emotional intelligence is cultivated in proximity to intimacy. It cannot be attained in isolation. The quality of our interpersonal relationships is both a product of and a contributor to our emotional well-being. Relationships can move us from academic exploration of awareness to a lived experience of it. They have the power to remove the veil of our self-deception. Only in the vulnerability of intimacy do we learn to see ourselves completely in the mirror of relationship. If we stay open and present to what we see mirroring back through the eyes of others, we are given the opportunity to understand how we are being perceived and received. Interpersonal relationships are not only a vehicle toward greater self-awareness; they are, perhaps, the whole point.

Committing to becoming awake and present in our relationships leads us to living more openhanded and inclusive lives. We see that no one is better and no one is less-than. Everyone is worthy, lovely, broken, beautiful, and significant—even if they don't know it. We are all pieces of the whole. And when any of us commits to doing our own inner growth work, there is a little less work for others to do. When we heal, we help others heal too.

Reflections

1. How have you seen your type in lower awareness sabotage your relationships? What was the cost?

2. Think of a time when you approached an important relationship from a place of higher awareness. How did the relationship benefit?

3. What can you do today to help heal and restore a fragmented relationship?

4. Think of someone in your life you do not naturally like. What can you do today to start to get to know them better?

6

Decision-Making

Every time you make a choice you are turning the central part of you, the part of you that chooses, into something a little different than it was before.

C. S. Lewis

As much as we'd like to believe that we are logical and objective beings, every decision we make involves our history, our beliefs, our sensations, and our emotions. Even the most rational among us are being continually influenced by all these factors along with our bodily state. Research has shown that even judges in courtrooms make decisions that are unconsciously influenced by something as simple as whether they've had their midmorning snack.[1]

While most of us later *justify* our decisions with the use of reason, the decisions we *make* always involve our emotions. How we feel has a disproportionate influence over our choices. Research has shown that people with even a small amount of isolated damage in the central (or ventromedial) portion of the brain can retain the same IQ level they had prior to the damage occurring yet experience significant long-term defects to their emotional awareness and decision-making capabilities. It turns out that emotions and good decision-making are inextricably linked.[2]

As was mentioned in chapter 2, when we walk into our office or face making an important decision, there is no such thing as "leaving our emotions at the door." Although that was once a popular business axiom and still permeates many organizational cultures today, it's simply not possible. What's more, expunging feelings shouldn't be the goal. Our emotions are a deep well of insights for us. The key to having our emotions work for us instead of against us is to enhance our awareness of them. If we surface, observe, and metabolize our emotions, we are more capable of sustainable and wise decision-making. When we are unaware of our emotions, our decisions are much more likely to be biased, reactive, and shortsighted.

Our beliefs influence our thoughts, our thoughts inform our feelings, and our feelings lead to actions. All the while, much of our brain's emotional constructs are the result of bottom-up sensory perceptions through the interoceptive process (in other words, our gut instincts). Working with the Enneagram helps us raise our conscious awareness of what we sense, believe, think, feel, and do. By engaging in the work of self-awareness, we can create space for intentional choices instead of automatic reactivity, making conscious decisions instead of merely reacting out of our conditioning.

In this chapter, we're going to explore some of the common pitfalls of making decisions; knowing the kinds of problems we're prone to encounter will help us avoid them in the future. Forewarned is forearmed. Then we'll explore how each Ennea-type approaches decision-making, for better or for worse. As we'll see, each type's blessing is also often its curse. Eights, for example, have no trouble making decisions, wanting to tackle problems immediately and forcefully. Yet this can be their downfall if they jump in before they have all the facts or they fail to listen to the ideas and experiences of others. Nines often suffer from the opposite problem: they listen so much to other people's opinions and desires that they can become paralyzed and incapable of action. When it comes to developing our EQ and improving our ability to make the right decision at the right time and in the right way, we need to understand what our type's default mechanisms are and learn to transcend them.

Using the Enneagram in Your Decision-Making

To start, we must learn to observe where our automatic focus of attention goes and the feelings it provokes in us. Without that understanding, our choices are delusions because they aren't choices at all but predictable, conditioned patterns common to the shadows of our core Ennea-type. And when we are in the grip of our core Ennea-type, we are irrationally certain that we are making good choices. No one ever thinks they're making a bad decision when they are making it! This kind of irrational certainty can lead to catastrophic outcomes.

People are often bad at making rational decisions because in each moment we are influenced by multiple inputs that are constantly connected to how we feel. Following are four common illogical influences that muddy the waters of choice (there are, of course, many others):

- *Fear.* Each Enneagram type has a particular fear (which we will explore further in chapter 8). These fears show up in different ways at different times, but when we aren't aware of them, they can significantly influence our decision-making in detrimental ways.
- *Stress.* All of us feel stress (which we'll talk about in more detail in the next chapter). But too much stress can

severely impair our ability to make wise decisions as we operate with a sense of urgency, compulsion, or avoidance to attempt to relieve the feeling of stress.

- *Ego.* As we've been exploring, each Enneagram type is operating from their ego when they are in lower levels of awareness. From this place, each type believes they are right or tends to fall in love with their ideas or is overly concerned with image management. Ego diverts attention away from the decision and back toward the self.

- *Habits.* Everyone is hardwired for developing habits. It's a God-given feature of the human brain, allowing us to perform tasks such as driving a car (once we've become proficient) without having to think about what we are doing. It enables us to punch in our ATM code without having to try to recall the number. But it also works against our growing in awareness. The brain is a calorie hog, and if it can avoid doing any extra work, it will.[3] When we're unaware of how habits are influencing our decision-making, we have a proclivity to do what we've always done, without questioning it, to help us stay in our comfort zone where calories are stored for tasks we perceive as deserving of more complex thinking.

You may have a particular proclivity toward one of these pitfalls, but each Ennea-type is vulnerable to all of them. I'm not pointing these out for you to become self-critical or shamed. On the contrary, with empathy and self-compassion, you can become more honest with yourself so you can better understand the people and events around you. From the outset, release any shame that may arise in you when you contemplate these influences. Shame is the enemy of growth. But the good news is that shame cannot survive in the presence of empathy and self-compassion.

Dr. Robert A. Burton writes in his book *On Being Certain*, "We are raised believing that reasonable discourse can establish the superiority of one line of thought over another. The underlying presumption is that each of us has an innate faculty of reason that can overcome our perceptual differences and see a problem from the 'optimal perspective.'"[4] From an Enneagram perspective, each of us is under the delusion that we perceive things accurately from the vantage point of our type. And sometimes we do. But often we are feeding information through the storied filter of our dominant Ennea-type and then locking it in. It's as if we're playing *Who Wants to Be a Millionaire* by pressing the illogical Fear button or the Stress Reaction button or the Ego button. Or, my personal favorite, the Habits button.

When it comes to healthy decision-making, we are, first and foremost, in dire need of humility. Humility is the catalyst for willingly stepping back to acknowledge that our perspectives are limited, and our irrationality is unlimited. Regardless of our dominant type, we do not perceive reality as it is but only as it was useful to perceive it at some point in our past. According to the perceptual neuroscientist Beau Lotto, "in terms of the sheer number of neural connections, just 10 percent of the information our brains use to see comes from our eyes."[5] The other 90 percent is our brains trying to make sense of things through a myriad of other factors. In other words, none of us perceive objective reality, so it is foolish to think that we are rational decision-makers. This will always be true, but it's not as bleak as it may sound. Because once we loosen our grip on the delusion that we see and understand an objective reality, we can begin to transcend the limitations of our default perspectives.

From an Enneagram lens, we may infer that from the vantage point of our dominant Ennea-type, we are perceiving, at best, only 1/9 of the field of possibility. If we factor in Enneagram subtypes, we perceive only 1/27. If we include our repressed instincts, we perceive only 1/54 of the field.[6] In other words, until we do our growth work, we are stuck in the biased, self-limiting perceptions of the belief system of our Ennea-type because those beliefs served us at one time—but not because they were true or even accurate.

So again, if we are perceiving only a narrow picture of reality through our brain's limited prediction systems and our own personal histories, why do we often exhibit so much confidence in our decision-making abilities?

Let's step back here and focus on how we can begin to leverage the wisdom of the Enneagram to help us become more humble and better able to make balanced, fair, and holistically beneficial decisions. How can we begin to understand our natural approach to decision-making and then expand these perceptions to create better choices—a bigger field of possibility? In addition to learning to recognize the unconscious motivations and self-limiting beliefs of our dominant Ennea-type and then seeing how these factors are influencing us every day, we can also do some practical reflection by returning once again to the centers of intelligence (Body types, Heart types, and Head types) and what they have to offer us (doing, feeling, and thinking).

Remember, the Enneagram teaches that there are three basic ways of approaching the world, which we call the intelligence centers. While all of us are most naturally comfortable in one of these three triads, emotional intelligence comes from creating greater balance among all of them. For example, while Ennea-types Eight, Nine, and One are naturally more connected to physical sensations, everyone can improve their relationship to their own bodily awareness and their interoceptive signals. As Annie Murphy Paul writes in her extraordinary book *The Extended Mind*, "People who are more aware of their bodily sensations are better able to make use of their non-conscious knowledge." She goes on to say, "Sensing and labeling our internal sensations allows them to function more efficiently as our somatic rudder, steering a nimble course through the many decisions of our days."[7]

As you can see, we need to learn to become much more connected to our bodies. Our bodies, like our emotions, are a profound source of wisdom and insight. But this is true of all three of the centers of intelligence: we need to think with our minds, feel with our hearts, and trust our gut instincts.

Center of Intelligence	Action	Type
Body types	Doing	Eight
		Nine
		One
Heart types	Feeling	Two
		Three
		Four
Head types	Thinking	Five
		Six
		Seven

As you can see, each of the nine core Enneagram types starts with a dominant intelligence (doing, feeling, or thinking). That's the mode of understanding the world that just comes most naturally, like Fives (a Head type) making sense of things by gathering information, or Twos (a Heart type) interpreting the emotions all around them. However, those are strengths that can become crutches if we rely too heavily on the dominant center to the exclusion of the other ways of experiencing the world. Each Enneagram type also has what is called a "support" center, which is like a second-string team that we sometimes call into action to help our dominant center, and a "repressed" center, which is the one that needs the most development and work. That's the one our Ennea-type tends to ignore.

When we understand these, we can begin to learn not to overrely on our dominant intelligence and to intentionally engage with the other centers, thereby expanding our perception of what is possible and what would be most useful—situation by situation—to help us make better decisions.

When we speak about repressing one of the intelligence centers from an Enneagram perspective, we aren't suggesting its absence, merely observing its potential ineffectiveness. In other words, how much do we rely on or avoid using a particular intelligence center to make our decisions? And when we engage it, how helpful or distracting does that center become?

Each of us naturally overuses our dominant intelligence center. Part of our growth work, then, consists of trying to bring balance to these centers (some suggestions for how to do so are in the final chapter of this book). I cannot stress this enough: when it comes to living emotionally intelligent lives, creating balance is everything.

Enneagram Types and Decision-Making

Type One

In low awareness, Ones overrely on gut instinct (doing) to make their decisions, supported by feeling, and they repress thinking. This concept is often surprising to the One, and those who know them, because Ones seem to be thinking constantly (in fact, Ones can often look like Sixes, a Head type). However, Ones have a proclivity toward categorization more than most of the other types—things are either good or bad, black or white, left or right. Whereas everyone's brains are hardwired to save calories by quickly putting things into categories, Ones aren't as likely to step back and re-evaluate their rapid-fire evaluations.

In their gut, Ones believe they simply *know* what's what. They prefer to make decisions within the confines of the rules, and therefore nuanced thinking isn't easily deployed. The thinking that does consume them, however, is often unproductive in that it is directed at a perpetual cycle of self-evaluation and the evaluation of others as to whether they are measuring up to the internal standards that the One has set. In this lower state of awareness, the thinking never stops. Ones direct their energy toward thinking about how nothing quite measures up, including themselves, and also toward rationalizing decisions they've already made and actions they've already taken. This thinking is what drives the emotional vice of anger for Ones—an internal standing against reality compelled by a desire to change it. From this vantage point, the One is likely to be convinced of the right decision yet never really satisfied with the results that follow. And round and round they go.

In high awareness, Ones direct their thinking toward possibilities and creative solutions to problems. They don't actively seek to break the rules but are generally less concerned with them. They adopt an open posture and engage in active listening with those around them, no longer confident that they positively know the right way to do something. Perhaps the biggest shift that happens when Ones are highly aware is that they become willing to make decisions that may lead to failure. Freed from their former rigidity about needing every choice to be perfect, they become willing to take risks and learn from mistakes. They can refrain from berating themselves or others for anything that doesn't work out as hoped. Highly aware Ones understand that there is rarely a textbook choice to be made—the world is forever uncertain, and perfection doesn't really exist. When Ones understand and integrate this at a core level, they find serenity in their messy, unpredictable world and in the process become the type of decision-makers who get far better results than when they thought they *knew* every right choice.

Type Two

In low awareness, Twos overrely on feeling to make their decisions, and they repress thinking. Similar to Ones, this concept is often surprising to Twos as they report thinking constantly. But what they are primarily thinking about is other people. In a low state of awareness, type Two is ruminating about every facet of their relationships even when the people they are thinking about aren't aware that they're the focus of so much attention. Twos' thinking is motivated primarily by feelings: How much do other people love and appreciate me? How important am I in their lives? How can I get this person to like me? Ironically, the disproportionate amount of energy they give to maintaining a relationship score-card at all times for the important people in their lives ends up working against them. Twos cannot make thoughtful, balanced, and well-informed decisions as long as they remain so concerned with how they are being perceived, measuring their own sense of value by the opinions of others.

In high awareness, Twos use their feelings to turn inward and explore what is authentically going on inside of them. They discover what they truly want without worrying about meeting anyone else's approval. As they let go of their relationship scorecards, their thinking becomes unclouded and directed toward a more objective analysis. They are no longer as concerned with popular opinion as they are with the effectiveness and the "return on investment" of the choices they're making. No longer motivated to super-serve certain people, they are now able to approach more difficult decisions from a big-picture perspective, even if that decision means they won't win any popularity contests.

Type Three

In low awareness, Threes lead with feeling and repress feelings at the same time. As stated earlier, Threes are the most feeling type on the Enneagram, yet they have little *access* to their own personal feelings. They use feelings to quickly assess the interests of others and to imagine a future outcome. They simultaneously push aside their own feelings so that nothing interferes with taking decisive action in the direction that will please the most people and secure the most praise. Threes use thinking and doing equally to support the acknowledged feelings from which they lead. However, I personally suspect that doing has a slight edge over thinking for the less aware Threes as they can be quick to jump into action and even cut corners to get a rapid-fire result when under stress or pressure. This can sometimes lead to blame shifting when the decision they've made was wrong or they took too sharp a short-cut. Threes are the most image-conscious of all Ennea-types and, in lower levels of awareness, may distance themselves from failures at all costs.

In high awareness, Threes become introspective and mine the various, sometimes disparate, emotions they've been repressing. The more emotionally granular they become, the more they develop clarity about what it is they authentically want and why. They are less inclined to rush a decision or override the opinions of others in order to achieve a quick win. In this reflective, less achievement-driven state, they become more inclusive and learn to truly listen to others beyond their old habit of merely listening in order to assess what other people wanted from them. They are much less preoccupied with the optics of their choices and focus instead on values and integrity. From this posture, the field of possibility often expands for highly aware Threes. Instead of calculating which decision will make for the best headline, they scan for possibilities that are potentially more meaningful and sustainable in the long run, even if it means doing more work behind the scenes and without any obvious accolades.

Type Four

In low awareness, Fours depend almost exclusively on feelings to make their decisions, and they repress doing. Fours have more *access* to their own feelings than any other type on the Ennea-gram. This puts them in a favorable position for understanding the potential impacts that any particular decision could have on themselves and others. It also orients them toward projects and decisions that will have big effects because they crave depth and drama. However, what gets repressed from this level of awareness is the willingness to focus on little details or mundane decisions that also require their attention. Often, this neglect can undermine their success as they avoid handling the particulars that will enable the sustainability of any project or initiative they've been working on. With feeling in the driver's seat, the low-aware Four can often shift focus and priorities based on whatever feels strongest in them from moment to moment. This can lead to inconsistency, a lack of clarity, and frustration for their teams and stakeholders.

In high awareness, Fours surround themselves with people and structures that will help them process, validate, or challenge their feeling-driven choices. Appreciating the importance of excavating emotions to understand their origin, Fours in higher awareness investigate their options through reasoning and microtests to authenticate or delegitimize any oversized emotions that may have been pushing them toward one decision or another. Being less concerned with projecting a unique image or pursuing grandiosity, they're now content to sit in the mundane examination of pros and cons, charts, and graphs. While still valuing how they feel about something, they also now understand that ordinary data analysis can help them make better, balanced, informed decisions, even in instances when the best choice feels like the most boring of them all. And once the decision is made, they're willing to step into the sometimes-tedious tasks of implementation without complaint or feeling that the work is underutilizing their gifts.

Type Five

In low awareness, Fives put too much stock in thinking to make their decisions, and they repress doing. They are the pioneers of autonomous discernment and knowledge gathering. They are curious about the interrelatedness of all things, which enables them to bring a wealth of insights to any decision-making table. However, motivated to be competent and to avoid being overwhelmed by the demands of the world, Fives can sometimes withdraw into their heads to avoid their own feelings and relationship needs. From this posture of distant retreat, they may get stuck in overanalyzing even the most inconsequential choices presented to them and neglect to act in a timely fashion.

I once knew a Five who took three years to decide which new sofa to buy for her living room. She wouldn't pull the trigger until she'd been to every store and researched every option. Twice. Meanwhile, she would complain about the shabby state of her existing sofa time and again. She just couldn't go from analysis to action on something that for most other types wouldn't have taken nearly as long.

With a proclivity to isolate themselves in their mental processes, Fives often miss the opportunity to involve others in their decision-making, which could help push them forward if they allowed it.

In high awareness, Fives get out of their heads and grounded in their bodies. They open themselves up to realize that other people's decision-making processes, including the use of feeling and instinct, are equally valid ways to arrive at meaningful conclusions. They no longer withdraw from others to analyze alone, and they become more comfortable in our VUCA (volatile, uncertain, complex, and ambiguous) world. Knowing that it is impossible to de-risk every choice, they are willing to swing into action more quickly than before. They begin to feel free to place some bets on the future without fear of reprisals because they remain confident that even if they bet wrong, they will endure. Nothing is final.

Type Six

In low awareness, Sixes lead with thinking and repress thinking at the same time. At the center of the Head triad, they are among the most cerebral types on the Enneagram, and yet their thinking often gets stuck in unproductive loops that delay taking timely action or appropriate risks. Sixes, like Fives, are in their heads quite a bit and may be slow to decide something. However, unlike Fives, Sixes tend to prolong decisions, not through investigating but through questioning—playing devil's advocate and thinking out loud—as they try to work out all possible dangers. Sometimes what they say aloud isn't even what they really think; it's the contrarian point of view they need to voice just to see if they believe it. As we've explored, their goal is to alleviate the passion of fear through certitude. When difficult-to-acknowledge thoughts and emotions arise, they may project their fears onto others as an unconscious strategy for quieting uncertainty and reducing their anxiety over an important decision. When this inevitably fails, their anxiety may skyrocket and leave them in a quandary since fear and good decisions don't often play well together.

In high awareness, Sixes' thinking becomes more productive and less frenetic. They become more tolerant of risk and are therefore able to make decisions more quickly. While still maintaining analytical strength, their mental processes relax, and they are able to connect more fully with their heart and their gut. Somewhat ironically, this calmer and more balanced approach to decision-making creates greater clarity about the right choices to make, which leads to better outcomes. From this vantage point, the passion of fear eases through faith and courage in the face of uncertainty—not in finding certainty, which is what less healthy Sixes have been chasing. Sixes in high awareness realize that such certitude is impossible, and the quest for it only perpetuates the fear cycle. When fear does arise, the Six in higher awareness acknowledges it without feeling the compulsion to project the fear elsewhere.

Type Seven

In low awareness, Sevens lean too heavily on thinking to make their decisions, and they repress their feelings. Sevens in a state of low awareness trust only their own plans, seeing themselves as the creators of their own reality. They chafe against the limits of life, so they work hard to create their own destiny, deceiving themselves that they are freer than they are. They are easily frustrated when asked to stop and make organizational decisions because often any choice, and the process of decision-making itself, feels too constricting. These Sevens are easily frustrated because although the future ideal in their minds isn't a real option for them in the moment, or possibly ever, their egos keep deceiving them that their wisdom would be best applied to creating that imagined future rather than dealing with today and the decisions it requires. Therefore, they may be more comfortable deflecting decisions (though they will call it delegating) so they can get back to making abstract plans for the future.

In high awareness, Sevens stop inventing more and more choices. They begin to understand that there is wisdom that exists outside themselves, and the best way to become truly wise is to slow down and become open to receiving it. This means welcoming whatever life is bringing to them now rather than hastily moving forward to avoid possibly painful choices. When they align themselves to this reality, they begin to see themselves as capable of going with the flow and doing the work that presents itself, without circumventing challenges. This allows them to remain present to the decisions that need to be made now rather than neglecting what the present requires of them so they can chase after a future ideal. When healthy Sevens have experienced the limited choices of the present, they find true freedom *in* those limitations rather than believing they must be free *from* them. When this shift occurs, everyone starts to benefit from the high mental cognition and intelligence of the Seven, which leads to brilliant decision-making.

Type Eight

In low awareness, Eights bank only on gut instinct to make their decisions, and they repress their feelings. Similar to type One, they believe they know the right choice and the right way of doing things, though they can be much more impulsive than Ones. While they may assume they've made logical conclusions, in lower levels of awareness, their reactions are much more primal and visceral before any real contemplation or collaboration has happened. For important decisions, this can have dire consequences if their instincts prove to be wrong. What's more, even if they're right, their bulldozing tendencies may make others feel isolated and unimportant when Eights make choices of consequence without soliciting advice or listening to others' differing opinions. The more passionate or intense Eights feel at the point of decision, the more likely they are to be convinced that they are correct and, therefore, do not need input from their network of peers. This creates a lot of unnecessary risk and is motivated by an unconscious need to protect themselves from a perceived threat of being controlled or exploited in some way, even if no such threat actually exists.

In high awareness, Eights curb their impulses and reconnect to their softer, more tender emotions. Less guarded, they invite trusted others into the decision-making process. They're attentive to divergent viewpoints without defensiveness. Their natural desire for truth and justice becomes more informed and holistic, unfiltered by the drive for self-protection and control. They are now willing to admit to feelings of weakness and vulnerability in the face of uncertainty. While still retaining confidence in their abilities, they are much less prone to arrogance. This leads to less intense environments, not because the Eights are suppressing themselves but because they've embraced more of themselves—the hidden parts are revealed. When Eights can take that leap into the unknown, greater team dynamics and psychological safety follow closely behind. From a place of quieter strength, everyone's voices are heard and true collaborative decision-making wins.

Type Nine

In low awareness, Nines immerse themselves in doing things on behalf of others and repress doing things on their own behalf. At the center of the Body triad, they are the most body-based type on the Enneagram, yet their fear of becoming as big and powerful as they really are causes them to switch off their innate preference for action. Instead, they substitute comfortable routines and activities that pacify their relationships and themselves. When it comes to decision-making, low-aware Nines will always defer asserting their agenda to the will of their routine, their colleague, or the group. They will go to astonishing lengths to avoid making a choice that could upset someone, which would, in turn, upset themselves. They make choices that will preserve external and internal calm.

Decision avoidance will inevitably lead to decisions being made on their behalf, which may infuriate Nines who resent being overlooked or disagree with the decision they abdicated to others. However, in wanting to keep the peace, they will avoid expressing this anger and instead double down on the very strategy that led to this predicament. What this often looks like in practice is inaction and stubbornness. In this lower level of awareness, Nines are stuck between wanting to feel calm and not wanting to support a decision they disagree with. While they may give the appearance of support, they will refuse to follow through on tasks they seemed to promise they would do. Ironically, this can then lead to others feeling deeply frustrated with them for not doing their part—leading straight to the conflict the Nine was always trying to avoid.

In high awareness, Nines begin to advocate on their own behalf. They've learned that not making decisions *is* a decision—with often unfavorable results. They can identify what it is they truly want, and then act on it. Highly aware Nines are no longer reluctant to connect to the primal emotion of anger, using this emotion to drive themselves toward what they desire instead of the previous pattern of simply avoiding the things they didn't desire. They are grounded, centered, and willing to speak up, yet they still maintain a collective, collaborative mindset that factors in the impact to others of all of their decision-making. However, they are now willing to make tough and even unpopular decisions after having weighed all the data. This is a Nine in motion, almost appearing like an Ennea-type Three in their level of energy, drive, and determination. Self-aware Nines make brilliant leaders and decision-makers who own their power and do not procrastinate.

Decision-Making: From Low to High Awareness

If we can't rely on the accuracy of our own perceptions and if our choices are inseparably connected to our emotions, how then do we make consistently informed, considerate, productive choices from a place of high awareness? As I hope you're starting to see, the answer is rooted in our *mindset*.

The notion of mindset is entrenched in Carol Dweck's work on the theory of fixed and growth mindsets in children and how these reflect our rational mental processes, assumptions, and beliefs. Those with a fixed mindset see their traits and qualities as unchangeable—they can only play the hand they're dealt and nothing more. Those with a growth mindset, however, see the hand they've been dealt as the beginning, not the end. Such individuals are primed for learning and stretching themselves because they believe change is possible and are therefore willing to do the work.[8]

Our mindset is how we uniquely see situations, solve problems, make choices, and form and sustain personal relationships. Building a healthy mindset is, at its core, our ability to confront the assumptions we make in every facet of our lives. And the key to confronting these assumptions is to observe the influence that our emotions have on our discernments. When we don't allow ourselves to feel and understand our emotions, we are at most risk of getting caught in the net of the illogical influences mentioned earlier: fear, stress reaction, ego, and habits.

For example, the COVID-19 pandemic and the tumultuous political landscape in the United States and beyond produced an enormous array of subtle, and often heated, emotional experiences in people throughout the world. And understandably so. The fears, losses, and anger of living amid that volatility and divisiveness had impacts on people that are yet to be fully understood.

If you're at all like me, sometimes my emotions during the pandemic were not consciously experienced. I wasn't always fully aware of or connected to my inner experience. As a person who leads with Ennea-type Three, I sometimes find it challenging to slow down long enough to process my own feelings. When I had unacknowledged, difficult emotions just outside my field of consciousness, they had an adverse impact. On those days, I was a mediocre team player. I was closed off to new ideas, stressed, not the greatest listener, and maybe a bit unmotivated. In this state, I was inclined to make reactive, less considered decisions. Other times, when I chose to stop and perhaps go for a walk, I was able to reflect on what I was feeling and *why*. I could then surface the information that was embedded in my emotional experience, understand it, metabolize it, and move forward with clarity. On those days, I was capable of healthy decision-making despite the external conditions.

The point is this: what we *feel* plays a more significant role in our decision-making than anything we can possibly *think*, particularly when we aren't conscious of what we are feeling. Our mindset is profoundly *about* our emotions.

What, then, is the mindset we want to adopt? There are two mindsets we need to pay close attention to, which are more nuanced descriptions of the growth and fixed mindsets mentioned above: open and defensive. People with an *open* mindset seek out information, ideas, and solutions that can be tested. They see themselves and others more clearly. People with a *defensive* mindset, on the other hand, seek out information that will protect them from having to change their beliefs. They exclude from their sight anything that would challenge what they've already decided to believe.

Regardless of your dominant Enneagram type, assume that you are making decisions from a defensive mindset when you are in lower levels of awareness. That's because the entire structure of your Ennea-type is designed to defend itself and its way of interacting with the world (we will look at defensiveness in depth in chapter 9 of this book). In other words, it is inflexible. When we are in higher levels of awareness, however, we are capable of decision-making from an open mindset because we invite our emotional experiences into the conscious mind and become open to the diverse perspectives of the other eight Ennea-types. From this open mindset, we adopt an inclusive posture and can better access all three of the intelligence centers. And if we are intentional about inviting others with a different dominant intelligence center into our decision-making process, they become our teachers in learning to better access the intelligence centers we are less accustomed to engaging.

An Enneagram Four once told me how difficult it was for her to see her start-up nonprofit scale as it became more successful. On one hand, she was elated by the positive impact they were making in the communities in which they operated. On the other hand, scaling the business meant creating more systems, processes, and streamlining that sometimes caused her to want to resist some of the changes to protect her "baby." She shared that as the organization grows, she's had to take regular inventory of her emotions when experiencing an internal sense of resistance to a proposed change to evaluate if what she's feeling is because she honestly disagrees with what was proposed or if she's merely trying to defend something she spent so much time building herself.

This intentional stepping back to investigate feelings and question the beliefs underneath them has equipped her to understand when she has an open mindset and when she has a defensive mindset. As she's learned, having an open mindset doesn't make you endlessly agreeable. Open-mindedness doesn't mean you think every idea is worth trying. It means you can actively listen to diverse perspectives and consider new ideas without your ego getting in the way. As a Four, knowing that she naturally feels so deeply for the important work she does in the world, she has committed to intentionally surrounding herself with Head types and Body types as advisers to help ensure that she is equipped to see things she may have otherwise missed. She's not looking to completely de-risk every move (impossible) but to de-risk decisions from her own bias.

Understanding our emotions and the influence our bodily sensations have on them is the most important element of becoming better decision-makers. Start by simply paying attention to how you are feeling: Are you tired? Hungry? Melancholy from the gray weather? Once you've established that baseline, think about its impact: How are these feelings shaping your choices? Bringing conscious awareness to your emotional states and being honest with yourself and others are foundational for emotionally intelligent decision-making.

Reflections

1. Have you ever made a major decision that you regretted? What were you feeling at the time?

2. Where does your focus of attention go when you are faced with a decision of consequence? How has this helped you and hurt you?

3. Do you ever resist making decisions altogether for fear of upsetting someone? What is the outcome if/when you do this?

4. Commit to revisiting your decisions every time you know you've entered a feeling state that is different from the emotions you experienced at the time your decision was made. Would you make the same choice now or a different one?

7

Stress Management

The greatest weapon against stress is our ability to choose one
thought over another.

William James

Remember the story of my anxiety attack that I told in the introduction? As I was struggling to maneuver my car across lanes
of traffic and onto the exit ramp while dialing 911 and wondering
if I was about to faint (or die), I was thinking many thoughts. But
not one of those thoughts was about stress. In those panicked moments, panic itself wasn't on my mind. Only later, when I reflected
on this ordeal, did I begin to contemplate the stress I was under
and how distant I felt from it.

My body sounded an alarm that day. What felt embarrassing
and defeating in the moment (a story I thought I would never tell)
turned out to be a forcing function for good. My body (which
is actually more rational than my mind because it can process
more information and isn't subject to cognitive biases) issued a

wake-up call.[1] This was my chance to take notice of my somatic rudder, repressed feelings, and the misguided motivations that had me unconsciously believing a story that wasn't true. The internal signals I'd ignored testified to mushrooming levels of denied stress that fueled the story I was living. For me as a Three, the story was that my only real value lay in what I could achieve—that people wouldn't like me for just me but only for what I could do for them. So I believed that I needed to push personal feelings aside for another day, keep moving, keep performing, keep adding items on my to-do list, keep succeeding. The applause was my guide.

No matter what our personal experience has been with stress or anxiety, each of us is trying to navigate and manage the world with the useful but very limited resources that our Ennea-type provides to us. Unfortunately, we trudge along in this task without being able to properly access and balance the thoughts, feelings, and behaviors of the other eight Enneagram types. This is a central reason why we get overcome with stress at times—we are trying to process and solve life's problems from a singular vantage point (like the adage "When all you have is a hammer, everything looks like a nail"). However, when we grow our awareness, we grow our options. We loosen the chains of our type and begin to access and integrate the strengths and resources of the other Enneagram types.

There are numerous reasons, of course, why we experience stress in our lives. It would be unfair of me to try to distill it all down to a couple of key themes and then provide a panacea for suggesting how you can overcome stress once and for all. Such a solution does not exist, and you shouldn't trust any person, book, or workshop that claims it does. What I can point out, from an emotional intelligence perspective, is that we often experience stress because of the competing priorities in our lives. This can happen when our desires clash with the reality of our present situation (for example, when a type Eight attempts to assert control but is thwarted by someone who has more control than they do, or when a type Six is forced into a high-risk situation without the proper time to assess the dangers beforehand). In these stressful situations, our type's default programming kicks in. We react out of conditioning, which renders us unable to step back and evaluate the ways in which we are the source of our own anxiety. Here's a hint to help you reflect on that: the passion of your Ennea-type is the *cause* of almost all your anguish.

It's important to note that not all stress is bad; it serves a core biological function. When we are under attack, for example, our inborn, hardwired fight-or-flight responses kick in to protect us. However, high levels of chronic, unaddressed stress can have numerous adverse effects on our work, relationships, health, and even lifespan. If you're curious about the cost of stress in our workplaces, the American Psychological Association estimates that "550 million workdays are lost each year due to stress on the job" and that up to 80 percent of workplace accidents and more than 80 percent of doctor visits can be attributed to stress.[2]

What's particularly concerning is that stress is on the rise. A 2019 Gallup poll revealed that Americans are among the most stressed people in the world, reporting stress, anger, and worry at their highest levels in a decade—and that was before the 2020 global pandemic.[3] Since then, things have only gotten worse. A 2021 survey published by the American Psychological Association revealed that a majority of adults reported experiencing undesired weight changes since the start of the pandemic. Two-thirds said they were sleeping more or less than they wanted to. Nearly half of parents experienced a significant increase of stress in their lives, and many essential workers sought treatment from a mental health professional to help them navigate the stress they were forced to endure.[4]

Many other studies all point to the same conclusion: stress is skyrocketing and the impacts of it will be felt for generations to come and in ways that we can't even predict yet. This makes it essential that we learn to deal with stress in an emotionally intelligent manner. Thankfully, there are strategies that can help.

Flexibility, Tolerance, and Optimism

Stress is complex. It can be a product of many factors, and it isn't merely something to be "managed" (contrary to the title of this chapter). Instead, we must expand our resources, our capacity to cope with life's demands. From an emotional intelligence perspective, one way we can start to do this is by cultivating healthy levels of *flexibility*, *tolerance*, and *optimism* in order to be able to thrive when the stressors of life come our way. These three traits are the emotional intelligence subscales used in the EQ-i 2.0 system I use to determine how people deal with stress. As with all the different measures in the EQ-i 2.0 system, these are reliable and valid lenses through which to understand our EQ skills in this area.

Flexibility is about how we handle the unexpected. There are numerous lessons to be learned from our lived experiences throughout the pandemic, but surely flexibility should be one of them. I hope we all became more radically aware of the limitations of our Ennea-types as we tried to navigate the fear and uncertainty of the crisis using the same playbook we've always used. None of us could have been prepared for what happened in 2020, of course, and that is precisely the point. Each of us tends to be convinced of the efficacy of our strategies to assert control over the outcomes of life according to the programming of our Ennea-type—until something like a pandemic reminds us how little control we actually have.

When something like this happens, we face a choice: we can double down on our familiar tactics, or we can admit their shortcomings and our inability to control the world. Accepting our limitations helps free us from the stress that comes from trying to manage our stress. It allows us to step into the flow of life instead of trying to trudge against its currents. Getting into the flow adopts a posture of flexibility so that wherever the currents take us we can accept that it is precisely where we must go. It is not to give up our agency; it is to give up the lie of control.

Tolerance is about how we cope with the stress we experience. What do we do when we are in a stressful situation? Some fall to pieces at the slightest problem while others thrive under even intense pressure. Although it's true that stress tolerance comes more naturally to some Ennea-types, it's not so much an innate, immutable characteristic as it is a skill that we can develop in combination with our flexibility. As we learn to cultivate the proper amount of flexibility when faced with the unexpected, we create more tolerance for the things we cannot control. When this skill is developed, we maintain healthy levels of composure in stressful situations, not because we deny reality but because we accept it.

Optimism is having a positive outlook on life and assuming the best—or at least, not assuming the worst. Optimistic people experience setbacks and problems just like everyone else, but they believe they will bounce back. Genuine optimism is not a refusal to confront reality—Sevens, the consummate reframers of negatives into positives, should listen up here—but rather a conscious choice to believe that things generally work out for our good. It is a deliberate decision to hold on to hope. When we learn to be properly flexible, we find the right amount of composure. When we are composed, we can find reasons to be optimistic. In my view, healthy optimism is present in each of the nine Enneagram virtues, and when we glimpse the virtue of our Ennea-type, we tap directly into it. No pessimism or hopelessness can be found within the genuine experience of serenity, humility, authenticity, equanimity, nonattachment, courage, sobriety, innocence, or right action.

These three traits—flexibility, tolerance, and optimism—are scales to be balanced in order to help us handle stress and thereby enhance our emotional intelligence. In what follows, we'll see how these traits tend to play out in the nine Ennea-types. The average person can learn a lot about their approach to stress through the lens of the Enneagram. To get started, and to repeat what has been stated in various forms throughout this book, we need to learn to surface and understand our emotions. Returning to Annie Murphy Paul's work, we see how "the simple act of giving a name to what we're feeling has a profound effect on the nervous system, immediately dialing down the body's stress response."[5]

Each of us has certain natural strengths and limitations when it comes to dealing with stress. Wherever you find yourself at the moment on the stress odometer, keep coming back to naming your emotions. Naming our feelings is to emotional intelligence what breath is to life.

Enneagram Types and Stress Management

Type One

In low awareness

Flexibility: Ones can be quite inflexible because of their instinctual certainty that they know what is and isn't right. If something is out of step with their rigid expectations of the way the world should be, they become angry, though they try to hold in their anger from a belief that anger is bad. This anger, then, seeps out in the form of bitterness toward the way things are. Less aware Ones often try to appear unaffected by this resentment and may hold it to the point of potential self-implosion.

Tolerance: Ones see outward composure as good, so they make every effort to model this behavior. They may feel capable of maintaining composure even during highly stressful situations but generally aren't as good with their poker faces as they like to believe they are. This often shows up as frustration when someone doesn't follow the same rules or hold to the same beliefs they do. Ones also carry a false belief that their stress will dissipate once everything has been made right. So they carry on working endlessly to improve the world around them. This, of course, leads to chronic stress, anger, and self-criticism when they are unable to create an external reality commensurate with their own internal principles.

If they continue with these perfectionistic strategies, they may unconsciously take on some of the archetypical characteristics of a type Four, including melancholy, envy, and retreating into themselves.

Optimism: Ones may feel a sense of optimism about the future, but this experience is usually intertwined with an overreliance on their own personal competencies in solving problems, following rules, and doing the right things. From this perspective, Ones aren't optimistic but are confident in their own ability to improve reality. Many people perceive less aware Ones as anything but optimistic since Ones so often call attention to problems, engage in criticism, and focus on what's wrong.

In high awareness

Flexibility: Ones begin to loosen their grip on self-imposed ideals and get more comfortable with gray areas, while still retaining their ethics, as they learn to internalize different points of view and accept things the way they are. These Ones let go of a preoccupation with personal competency and allow themselves to take risks, even knowing they may perform badly if they try something new.

Tolerance: From this vantage point, Ones no longer direct energy toward attempting to repress anger (or turn anger into a more acceptable emotion). Instead, their anger gets acknowledged and eventually begins to dissipate as they accept life and all of its vicissitudes. Freed from the preoccupation of withholding anger, Ones actually become less angry, able to temper the chaos around them without adding to it.

Optimism: Highly aware Ones understand that perfection isn't up to them and that there's loveliness to be found in everything. This helps them to calm the inner critic and all of its chronic stress. Their bodies relax from no longer resisting life, and they become more spontaneous, open, and cheerful, truly hopeful about what the future will bring.

Type Two

In low awareness

Flexibility: Less aware Twos may feel very flexible as they tend to bend over backward to help and serve others. However, this isn't as much flexibility as it is an impulse to please. There can be an emotional rigidity about what type of help Twos will give, and they may actively resist anyone else stepping in to assist or offer an alternative solution to a problem since this may diminish their usefulness in their own minds. This belief may add to the experience of chronic stress, if only unconsciously, as so much mental energy is directed toward evaluating where they believe they rank in each of their relationships.

Tolerance: Twos may feel a need to cultivate and demonstrate an image of being helpful, giving, and supportive. However, when this persona fails to bring about the emotional return on investment that is expected from their efforts, they may suddenly take on the characteristics of an archetypal type Eight and become aggressive and domineering. These Twos appear very much on edge and can lash out at others if they feel unappreciated or unloved.

Optimism: They may approach optimism through a lens of self-importance, elevating their own positive qualities and repressing negative thoughts and feelings. Being conscious of their personal image, they focus their attention on befriending others. This may often look like a warm, sunny optimism, which is pleasing but not necessarily sincere. Maintaining this image takes a lot of energy, which adds to Twos' experience of chronic stress over time. However, because they want to hold a positive outlook about what they can contribute, they may repress any feeling of stress until it explodes in seismic proportions.

In high awareness

Flexibility: These evolved Twos are flexible enough to freely allow people to care for them instead of compulsively looking out for others. Pride and shame give way to self-acceptance and a healthy self-confidence that isn't dependent on anyone's approval. They are aware of their own wants and desires, which adds up to creating a truer flexibility in them since they now have greater capacity to care for themselves and others, as needed, without overindulging or overextending themselves. Pride is gone and receptivity takes its place.

Tolerance: They release their grip on needing to appear helpful and are now more present to their own emotional experience. From here, there is a visible depth of authenticity that shines through to the world, that feels true and real. Instead of constantly pouring themselves out, they can direct their attention inward and connect with any painful emotions they've previously avoided through frenetically overextending themselves. They are now able to name their feelings in the face of stressful situations, helping them to stay grounded and present.

Optimism: These Twos embody a genuine humility that enables them to accept things and people just as they are—not better, not worse. This is an important evolution for type Twos. Their optimism is no longer contingent on whether they are indispensable to important people. Instead, it emerges from an understanding that things are unfolding according to a plan without the need for their intervention in others' lives. Stress is now significantly diminished by understanding that they can join in with all of creation without carrying the weight of it.

Type Three

In low awareness

Flexibility: These Threes may feel flexible in that they tend to be willing to take on more and more work while maintaining a belief that they have everything under control. They also take many shortcuts in their drive to look successful, aiming to accomplish as much as possible. However, because this mindset is fueled by a need to appear successful at all costs, they are actually imprisoned by the never-ending quest to win the approval of others in order to feel a sense of personal worth. Unfortunately, when they do achieve this feeling, it doesn't last, ebbing away as quickly as the round of applause that generated it. In chasing after the cheers, they tend to stand center stage and neglect to give credit where credit is due, leading to resentment over time from the people they most depend on.

Tolerance: Appearing successful includes making an outward show of remaining fully composed in the face of mounting pressures. This is a particularly dangerous place to stay for very long because prolonged image management requires repressing any feelings that would suggest not having it all together. Behind the scenes, when Threes' relentless performance mixes with unacknowledged emotional exhaustion, they may take on the archetypal characteristics of type Nine and withdraw into narcotization behaviors such as binge-watching shows, overeating, overexercising, or binge drinking. In this way, they attempt to deaden any awareness of what's really going on inside.

Optimism: Threes tend to be confident in their ability to overcome obstacles, painting a picture of limitless possibilities for others. They often navigate changing terrain with unwavering precision, suggesting that they saw around all the corners before they actually had. This builds confidence in Threes' ability to lead others through difficult circumstances. Underneath the exuberant exterior, however, less aware Threes may be living in fear that someone will find out they are faking it, at least a little, and that they don't necessarily feel the certitude they are projecting. This belief perpetuates a type of *forced* optimism as they are unable to admit feeling defeated even when they are. They cling to their personal competency to maintain a sense of optimism because at their core they embrace a false belief that they are valued only for their success and nothing more.

In high awareness
Flexibility: They accept the finitude of time and attention. They embrace the limits to what they can, or even should, try to accomplish. By saying no to new projects and more side hustles, they

create genuine flexibility in their schedules and can give their undivided attention to things they truly care about. No longer trying to multitask means no longer cutting corners or placing unrealistic demands on others to drive their personal agendas. Upon completion of high-profile projects, they effortlessly step from center stage and direct attention to what others contributed to that success.

Tolerance: They step back and evaluate potentially stress-producing problems with logic and pragmatism. Their focus of attention shifts from appearing to have it all together to ensuring that any outcomes will be beneficial to all involved. They become more attentive to the group, more loyal to colleagues and employees, and more considerate of diverse perspectives. This allows them to consider multiple scenarios in a given situation, bolstering a more informed opinion. Whereas they once only pretended to feel composure in the face of stress, they now genuinely do experience calm in difficult circumstances.

Optimism: Grounded in authenticity, their leadership becomes exponentially more effective as they willingly slow down, seek advice, involve the group in decisions, and honestly express any potential pitfalls they may see. This open and candid approach elevates a sense of psychological safety and trust in group members, who perceive that Threes will seek to understand uncertain circumstances and navigate them thoughtfully, together, and without cutting corners—no more "fake it till we make it" optimism. This is a truer optimism, one that humbly acknowledges threats and unknown variables, recognizes Threes' own limitations, and stays with problems long enough to find sustainable solutions. The future is still something these Threes believe in; they just no longer believe it's a future they are solely responsible for creating themselves.

Type Four

In low awareness

Flexibility: Unaware Fours are guided by an internalized false belief that their uniqueness will compensate for their sense of lacking. They seize upon their individuality as the most important thing about them, believing they are more flexible than other people because they claim not to care what the group wants or thinks. This is a mirage, however, because Fours often agonize quite deeply when they do not fit in the way others do. While their commitment to individuality can lead to tremendous creativity and beauty in how they see into the depths, it can also lock them into an inability to see the beauty on the surface. So when asked to participate in tasks that feel ordinary and routine, they may be less willing to pivot and become reliable partners for work that they deem to be less important. Instead of just rolling up their sleeves and showing up every day (which is a beautiful thing to do), they may distract themselves with new imagined possibilities at the expense of accomplishing what needs doing that day.

Tolerance: They are naturally aware of their emotions and can usually perceive the feelings in others. They may hold on to their emotions longer than necessary, particularly powerful feelings such as sadness, which are all rooted in the passion of envy. The personal strength of connecting with and understanding the depths of their own emotional experiences is a critical part of self-awareness that many other types covet. However, for the Four, their sense of self is often intertwined with these ever-changing emotional experiences in which they conflate their truest identity with whatever feelings they're having in the moment. When stress and pressures arise, others may experience these Fours' emotional reactions as all-pervading and dramatic. If stress persists, Fours may take on the characteristics of type Two, becoming overly enmeshed in other people's business or acting a bit prideful about when and how something should be done.

Optimism: They tend toward idealism—romanticizing a past ideal that was never quite true and projecting that ideal onto a future picture that will never quite get painted. At times, this can look like optimism as they are often brilliant at sharing a vision of all that could be possible. However, they just as often find themselves stuck in a melancholy about what isn't. Depending on subtype, the expressions of this type may vary significantly. Fours who have a dominant Self-Preservation instinct may appear cheerful and optimistic since they carry a burden of believing that it is their job to be long-suffering. Fours with a dominant Social instinct often appear much sadder since they tend to go deep into their pain. And Fours with a dominant One-to-One instinct seek compensation for their suffering and, therefore, can be quite intense and appear more Eight-ish. What is common is that all three of these subtypes of less healthy Fours suffer in their hearts because of the unnecessary comparisons being made in their minds—that there actually *is* an ideal (untrue) and that someone *else* has it (untrue) and they don't.

In high awareness

Flexibility: Fours in higher awareness learn to loosen their grip on the uniqueness of their ideas as a primary source of their identity. This allows them to be more accepting of sometimes simpler and more practical contributions from others when that's what the situation calls for, espousing a new flexibility in their relationships with others. They also stop imagining an ideal experience that will finally help them to feel settled inside because they're already grounded and settled in the here and now. This creates more elasticity in their lives because they are no longer singularly focused on the idealized and can happily get involved in the mundane.

Tolerance: The comparison chatter in healthy Fours' heads dissipates, and they are free to engage life with a new levelheadedness because they are no longer concerned with determining who has it better or worse than they do. This significantly reduces the number of oversized emotions that previously felt all-consuming. Big feelings still come, but then they depart just as quickly. Emotions are now understood to be merely weather patterns that change from day to day. No feeling is permanent. This newfound appreciation of the impermanency of emotions (and everything else, really) helps Fours enjoy a more steady, internal calm in the face of external pressures.

Optimism: Fours in high awareness become much more grounded in their bodies and the present moment. Tethered to realism, they cast their visions and explore the depths of possibility without getting swept away by emotional currents of sadness or shame when hoped-for possibilities don't materialize. Optimism looks more like joining others in the everyday tasks and routines of life than it involves fantasies about ideals. Fours now know that they are always connected to the divine, a vital part of the whole of life, and that nothing was ever missing. In the face of potential stress and external pressures, they trust that they have all they need, they belong, and they are steadfast. Optimism comes with the knowledge that they are already equipped to be happy—if they want to be.

Type Five

In low awareness

Flexibility: While Fives can sometimes appear flexible due to their undemanding demeanors, they do more energy budgeting than any other Ennea-type. In lower levels of awareness, they are computing what any request of their time, attention, and other resources will *cost* them. So while they may change plans or pivot directions when asked and without much outward expression of irritation, they are constantly calculating what this means for them. In other words, flexibility itself is planned. A friend who identifies as a Five told me, "I would almost say I'm not flexible at all because if I know I'm going to need to be flexible, I have to prepare for it by getting quality time for myself beforehand." Another Five said she tends to be flexible in the sense that she'll allow someone else in the group to choose the restaurant or the movie, but any abrupt changes to the plan can hit her hard. "I'll have one way planned, something interrupts that, and then I mentally recalculate to reset the routine, schedule, budget, etc." (When she told me this, my mind's eye immediately pictured my car's GPS that repeatedly tells me, "Recalculating . . . recalculating" every time I take an unexpected turn.) Fives may pivot, but they are more *aware* of the pivot than other types. In other words, being easygoing and being flexible aren't necessarily the same thing.

Tolerance: Fives tend to remain quite composed and in control of their emotional expression. If anything, Fives in lower levels of awareness may be too composed at times. In high-intensity situations where fight, flight, or freeze signals are triggered, Fives may freeze and pass it off as quiet confidence and composure in the face of chaos. However, where there is a fear of being or appearing incompetent or uninformed, the internal dialogue in the mind of a Five is anything but tranquil. Their thinking goes into overdrive, analyzing every angle of a problem and constructing a plan to protect themselves next time. This isn't a bad thing in and of itself, of course, but overdone composure for Fives can be a way of withholding the expenditure of energy. And if they get stuck in too much controlled thinking, it can lead them to retreat from situations that actually demand their full presence. Under prolonged stress and pressure, Fives may unconsciously take on archetypal characteristics of Sevens, becoming almost frenetic and overwhelmed with thinking, when what others actually need from Fives is embodied action, not agitated contemplation.

Optimism: As a Head type, Fives are unconsciously attempting to mitigate fear by pulling things apart in their minds and reconstructing them again. They don't naturally trust that everything will be all right unless they have scrutinized every possible problem and solution. This isn't to say that all Fives are pessimistic, but most bend toward trying to be *realistic*. For most Fives, being realistic means measuring situations fully so they can plan properly. To do anything less means lacking control—and any perceived lack of control, or an encroaching fear of being caught unawares, escalates fears about the future. Fives in lower levels of awareness are far too consumed with *knowing* to leave any real room for trusting or hoping. Fives, like their neighbor the Six, may not understand why optimism would be a helpful pursuit. Optimism doesn't feel safe. However, at times there may be an overly optimistic reliance on their own knowledge and self-sufficiency.

In high awareness

Flexibility: In high awareness, there is more balance between the thinking, feeling, and doing centers. From here, Fives spend less time analyzing the energy costs of changing plans or feeling the need to be fully prepared. Freed from those preoccupations, they are able to get into action more quickly—even when something comes at them unexpectedly. By getting out of their heads they actually feel more energized since much of what consumes energy for Fives is engaging in the mental gymnastics of constantly trying to conserve energy. The more they allow themselves to go with the flow, the more they demonstrate to themselves that they have all the energy they need. Spontaneity has not overwhelmed their resources the way they previously feared. Fives in this higher level of awareness retain all their wonderful, measured, precision-engineered capabilities but are now also open, agile, and accepting of uncertainty.

Tolerance: While tolerance for less healthy Fives is rooted in a natural detachment from fully feeling their emotions and a need to present as competent and in control, in higher levels of awareness, emotions are felt fully and freely in the heart and there is less concern with appearing competent. Fives adopt a more open, receptive posture toward others and all the beautiful messiness that relationships bring. This freedom from aloofness helps the Five to feel more alive and in the moment. From here, the Five is less measured and planned and more grounded in the body and not just the head.

Optimism: In higher levels of awareness, Fives become less attached to information as a strategy for safety. They are less analytical about past events as a means to accurately forecast the future, and they are more comfortable with not knowing what may come their way. They retain their superior mental calculations but are no longer reliant on them for mitigating fears; they've learned to accept that no amount of deconstruction, reconstruction, analysis, or planning has ever really kept them fully safe. Certainty has always been an illusion, and unpredictable moments help make life wonderful. Healthy Fives relax in the knowledge that they are inseparable from the divine, that they have been brought safely to this moment, and that they can now find comfort in the hope of whatever will be. For Fives, optimism is exhale.

Type Six

In low awareness

Flexibility: Sixes may struggle with flexibility if they haven't had the proper time to question or challenge a particular course of action. Rooted in distrust of themselves and others, they look for assurances from well-developed processes and/or certain authorities, institutions, or belief systems. Finding confidence, even dogmatism, outside themselves is their preferred way to eliminate the fear their own minds experience in the face of relentless uncertainty. Sixes in lower awareness may think of themselves as flexible in that they want to explore multiple scenarios until they've reached what feels like a good solution to something. However, they engage in this effort in the pursuit of absolutes, looking always for definitive certainty. One Six I spoke to said, "I'm open to lots of possibilities for solutions, but once I've locked in on a way to do something, not doing it that way is very difficult." All Sixes tend to be fairly rigid about their particular way of trying to make the world feel more predictable, and their strategies rarely leave much room for going off script. Sixes who haven't yet discovered their courageous faith aren't living a flexible existence.

Tolerance: Phobic Sixes may tend toward higher levels of tolerance on the outside, particularly around certain authority figures, while feeling overwhelmed with fear and distrust on the inside. Counterphobic Sixes, however, often don't experience conscious fear on the inside but can appear much less composed on the outside as they tend to exert anger or project intensity in the face of threats. Regardless of subtype, Sixes in lower levels of awareness are often restless and unsettled, unable to quiet their thoughts and persistent questioning. They can be contrarian, their reactivity paradoxically escalating the very chaos they're trying to mitigate. Under prolonged stress or pressure, the Six may take on archetypal characteristics of an unaware Three, becoming more afraid of failure and exceedingly busy.

Optimism: When things are working out according to plan, Sixes in lower levels of awareness may feel a sense of optimism. After all, the very act of challenging assumptions, questioning decisions, and looking around corners will alleviate some fear and create a sense of confidence in the plans they are making. This uncanny ability to anticipate worst-case scenarios, always knowing exactly where the exits are, is a gift to us all (especially those of us who've never listened to the flight attendant's instructions on what to do in case of a water landing). But the reason for this superpower isn't optimism. I don't want to call it pessimism either. I think it is better explained as a misplaced desire to have the security and support they've gone without most of their lives. Less aware Sixes carry with them the self-doubt that comes from not having received the guidance they needed as young people; no one told them where the exits were or what to do in case of a water landing, so they had to find out on their own. And they won't rest until they're sure they've identified each and every possible survival strategy.

In high awareness
Flexibility: In higher levels of awareness, Sixes are willing to place some bets and take managed risks without succumbing to excessive fear about possible consequences. As Sixes learn to trust themselves, they become more flexible because they now possess the courage to act despite doubts or uncertainty. While they still

may feel convinced that their plan is the best plan, they demonstrate a greater willingness to try a different course of action should someone suggest it. There is now an inner balance, a melding of due diligence and "whatever will be, will be." While still hardworking and responsible, they are now much more trusting and relaxed. They can move from a "plan and act" approach to a "test and learn" philosophy, embodying what Winston Churchill meant when he said that "failures aren't fatal."

Tolerance: Higher awareness for Sixes means more courage. It does not mean that fear has forever vanished but that they're no longer consumed by it. Faith and courage move to the fore, mitigating fear and cowardice. I think the spiritual dimension may be of even greater importance for Sixes' growth journeys than for the other types. Although all types fear something, Sixes just fear. And no one can think or move forward with any clarity when locked in the grip of fear. Fear produces the freeze, fight, or flight response, none of which lead to inner calm or composure. Faith is the antidote—not faith in systems, politics, or institutions but faith in the divine, which brings order to chaos and is a spiritual guide even when no earthly guide can be found. Sixes in high awareness often have deeper levels of spiritual engagement, understanding the truth that nothing, not even death itself, can destroy the essence of who they are.

Optimism: When a Six finds hope, it is a truly beautiful thing. Dominant in thinking and with a gift for asking pointed questions, Sixes make wonderful partners in life and business. They are the yin to the yang of those who may be naturally reckless. (If your leadership team at work is made up of mostly Threes, Sevens, and/or Eights, add a Six to the mix ASAP!) When Sixes begin to heal from their childhood wounds, they can rediscover the kind of courage that only comes from faith. On solid footing, their questioning shifts from trying to avoid catastrophes to exploring new possibilities—from prevention to enablement. Sixes operating out of this higher level of awareness are able to experience hopefulness in the middle of uncertainty. They've accepted that nothing is certain and they need not expend so much mental energy trying to control the outcomes in life. Even when they were without tangible guidance and support, they made it through hard things. And they have no reason to doubt they will make it through again next time.

Type Seven

In low awareness

Flexibility: In lower awareness, Sevens can appear quite flexible in that they genuinely seem up for just about anything. They often have high FOMO (fear of missing out) and have a proclivity to accept just about every interesting invitation they receive. If, however, the invitation is to an event or project that feels restrictive or understimulating, Sevens will avoid committing. By avoiding any commitments that seem boring or restrictive, Sevens are responding to their fear of being trapped in deprivation. What may look like flexibility is actually driven by fear. Sevens gravitate toward new experiences because they seek stimulation and enjoyment above all else. When this is happening, Sevens aren't flexible at all—they are mentally fixated on planning for pleasure and inspiration while avoiding restrictions.

Tolerance: Sevens are often extroverted and unreserved. They tend to be playful and, in lower levels of awareness, may sometimes give the impression that they aren't disciplined or taking things seriously enough. Wanting to experience a little bit of everything, they're constantly scanning the horizon and skipping from one thing to another. The more they operate this way, the more distracted and fatigued they become. When this continues, and when stress and pressure start to build, they may take on the archetypal characteristics of type One, becoming rigid, micromanagerial, and resentful of things that haven't gone according to plan. This vacillation between noncommitment and perfectionistic rigidity can leave those around them frustrated and confused.

Optimism: Sevens are known for their optimism. It can be quite contagious! I've met a few Sevens who when asked their type have responded with total jubilation, "I'm a SEVEN with a SEVEN WING!" I've always thought that if I could choose a type to be, I would be a healthy and aware Seven (though I must admit that I've been in full Three mode when I've thought this—picturing everyone gravitating to my joyful disposition, listening to me craft masterful stories while hanging on my every word). But the cost of overdone optimism for the Seven is, essentially, missing much of what life brings—even the good stuff. By constantly reframing negatives into positives while excluding information that conflicts with the world they've created in their minds, Sevens are left with future-focused tunnel vision. This way of framing the world means they are unable to fully absorb what is happening in the moment— the positive and the negative—for their focus of attention is always looking beyond what they are experiencing right now.

I was once at an Enneagram conference where a Seven whose kids were grown shared that when recently looking through old photos of their lavish family vacations, she was bothered by how fuzzy those memories were for her. She wanted to know why she remembered so little of them. The answer moved her from the passion of gluttony to the virtue of sobriety at an astonishing pace when the facilitator said, "Because you were never really there." She'd lived her entire, fun, wonderful existence in the future—miles away from the experiences she'd spent her whole life planning.

In high awareness

Flexibility: In higher levels of awareness, Sevens become more mentally flexible in that they are willing to undergo experiences they may find unpleasant or restrictive if doing so will benefit others. They become much less self-interested and freer to truly go with the flow without obsessive planning to avoid being trapped in discomfort. Healthy Sevens are able to sit in the discomfort of a situation and allow the emotions that are associated with it to be fully experienced, knowing that any displeasure will evaporate over time. They are willing to slow down and be fully present wherever they are without latching on to only the most exciting events or people. This is true flexibility—a willingness to be in the here and now.

Tolerance: In higher levels of awareness, Sevens become a bit more temperate and focused. Less distracted by what *could be*, they are content to face what *is*. While still retaining their entrepreneurial mindset, their demeanor becomes more settled, consistent, and accepting of difficult truths. They are more balanced and less likely to vacillate. They still maintain their naturally friendly and sociable approach to life but not at the expense of allowing the full spectrum of emotional experiences to affect them. It is quite beautiful to see a Seven who has learned to feel sadness without fear.

Optimism: Sevens also become more appropriately optimistic. They are still inspirational and expectant but without the need to reframe reality or flee from pain. They now understand that pain is a part of life—sometimes a helpful part of life—and that there is no risk of suffering taking them captive forever. But they are now free to suffer toward greater levels of consciousness (which we'll explore in the next chapter) and can accept other people's suffering without the compulsion to help them look on the bright side. This acceptance of reality with all its unpredictability frees Sevens to abandon the frenetic optimism they've used as a tactic for excluding uncomfortable truths and to find genuine hope that all will be well and they will be taken care of. This mature optimism stems not from an imagined utopia but from a deep trust that life is unfolding according to a certain design. Sevens no longer need to rely on their own plans to feel safe.

Type Eight

In low awareness

Flexibility: Less aware Eights may disregard rules and the opinions of others. Dominant in gut intelligence (Body types), they have a proclivity toward believing they *know* the right way of doing things regardless of what others may think. While this freedom from caring about other people's opinions may in some ways resemble flexibility, it's actually an almost defiant rigidity. Eights too often deny themselves the opportunity to learn from others. However, when their intense determination is matched by an opposing position from someone they respect, they can be willing to head in a direction different from their own. When Eights trust other leaders, they can be somewhat flexible. If they don't trust the leadership, they may take over and plow through however they see fit in order to ensure that things get done the *right* way.

Tolerance: Less aware Eights can be intense and intimidating. They are forceful, particularly when things feel chaotic, inefficient, or unfair in some way. The decisive, take-charge attitude Eights adopt when they are stressed can be helpful in times of crisis, but in day-to-day life, it can feel unnecessarily controlling and domineering to those with quieter dispositions. Eights may also "poke the bear" from time to time in order to stir up a bit of conflict. Conflicts bring out the truth, and there's nothing Eights covet more than knowing the truth, the whole truth, and nothing but the truth. While this can be threatening to others, conflict feels like connection to Eights. However, when this tactic fails them and prolonged periods of stress set in, Eights may adopt the archetypal characteristics of type Five, becoming withdrawn and fearful.

Optimism: Less aware Eights are confident to a fault. In this way, they are perhaps optimistic about their ability to get things done and get them done the right way. But this is a "might makes right" mindset, a "winner takes all" sensibility that leaves nothing to chance or wishful thinking. Eights get into action faster than any other Ennea-type and rely on strength and power to affect the world, believing that they are owners of the truth. And their truth is that the world is unjust and unfair; they should never give away their power lest they be taken advantage of. This is not true optimism as much as a tendency to believe that Eights can only trust themselves to stem the tide of evil or get the job done.

In high awareness

Flexibility: Healthy Eights relax their intensity as they learn to consider the possibility that while their gut is a reliable source of information, it isn't the only source. They adopt a newfound humility that includes acknowledging they may not be right and a greater appreciation for diverse perspectives. Here, they discover true flexibility as they learn to go with the flow instead of asserting control. Recognizing that there is often more than one right way to do things, they open up to more possibilities—a receptiveness they may have once viewed as weak but which, somewhat ironically, strengthens them. Strength is achieved by releasing control and taking in a wider breadth of information and insights without fear that their slower, more inclusive approach is anything but inspiring and positively well-rounded.

Tolerance: Eights with greater awareness possess a quieter strength and more welcoming presence. They connect to softer emotions and become more outwardly tender and supportive. No longer fearing being controlled, they aren't quite so quick to take control of situations, and they become more collaborative and open. From this vantage point, Eights exude an unobtrusive confidence that has no need to fight or be right. They've let their guards down and are now able to properly think and feel before acting (integrating all three intelligence centers). They even willfully make themselves a bit smaller to help others grow bigger.

Optimism: More aware Eights are every bit as concerned with matters of truth, justice, and fairness as they always were. However, they release the false notion that they are the sole owners of those values. From here, they open their minds to a wider field of possibilities since they are now able to really listen and hear diverse perspectives. There is a brightness and a fresh sense of optimism when Eights understand they can trust other people to desire and work toward what is right; they are not alone in the quest for a better world. By accessing more viewpoints, Eights are actually closer to truth than they were before—safer and more hopeful than when they relied on sheer muscle to bend the world to their will. By releasing the false belief that they ever really had control or needed to take control, they can move forward more humbly and vulnerably, trusting in the universal truth that all of life is unified through the love of the divine. No amount of self-assertion from Eights could ever change that.

Type Nine

In low awareness

Flexibility: Less healthy Nines overdo flexibility while being one of the most stubborn types on the Enneagram. On the inside, they may be thinking no, but to others they are communicating yes—all in an effort to avoid rocking the boat. This superficial yielding to others may appear to be flexibility, but it has no agency. It's passivity or avoidance. Ironically, Nines in lower awareness are famously stubborn because although they say (or at least imply) they support someone else's plan or idea, they may not carry out whatever implied agreements have been reached. They manifest a particularly low energy for completing tasks they don't want to perform. This, of course, often leads to interpersonal conflict—the very kind of relationship divide that the Nine was trying so hard to avoid by appearing to be flexible. It can also lead to practical challenges such as scheduling conflicts that arise from allowing themselves to be double-booked. From this vantage point, Nines conflate self-forgetting with flexibility.

Tolerance: They are often cool and collected on the surface. Having gone to sleep to intensity and anger, they've adopted strategies for keeping the inner and outer waters calm. In this lower level of awareness, composure is partially the product of having made themselves smaller than they are—somewhat undetectable. Underneath, however, there may be a bubbling anxiety about how long their strategies for merging with routines or other people's agendas will satiate. Unconsciously, Nines may not believe they are a big enough container for their own inner rage. Like type Sevens who fear that if they recognize their sadness it might never leave them, Nines fear that if they ever connect to their anger it will consume them. Nines may adopt the archetypal characteristics of type Six (over-questioning and paranoia) as they become preoccupied with strategies for managing this fear.

Optimism: In lower levels of awareness, Nines may adopt an "everything is fine" posture. Driven by a somewhat compulsory need to have a positive outlook, they tend to avoid things that could demand too much from them or threaten to disrupt their peace in order to hold to their go-with-the-flow mindset. While this demeanor can make them incredibly easy to get along with, it is not true optimism, which is hopeful about the future but not evasive about the realities of conflict or change. Such false positivity can perpetuate the self-forgetting tendencies of the Nine, if the reason that everything is fine is because everything demanding, particularly the work they need to do within themselves, is being avoided. For as long as the Nine is far from themselves, their optimism is actually narcotizing.

In high awareness

Flexibility: On the surface, healthy Nines may actually appear less flexible than unhealthy Nines because they are willing to show up and lead. They are unafraid to make tough decisions and ruffle some feathers in the process. Instead of merely going along to get along, they get in touch with what is truly important to their own agenda. When they assert their own will, it's not a passive resistance but a clearly communicated no to the things that would cost them themselves. These Nines have discovered that real flexibility cannot exist without first having limits. With appropriate boundaries established, Nines have lines drawn in the sand from which they can choose to flex—a place from which they can say either yes or no.

Tolerance: In higher levels of awareness, Nines actually become less concerned with being composed because they know the world will not end if their tranquility is tested. They've connected to their anger and their agendas, and they will express themselves honestly, directly, and without apology. If something provokes a righteous anger in them, they are better able to express it freely and without fear that any ensuing conflict will spell the end of their relationships. They are now present and clearheaded about what is important to them. And they are expressive with a much fuller range of emotions.

Jo, a Nine friend of mine who was experiencing a lot of bodily discomfort, went to get acupuncture several times. After a few visits, the acupuncturist told her to find a quiet place, outside and far away from everyone she knew, where no one could hear her. "I want you to then scream at the top of your lungs until you're out of breath or your voice goes," the acupuncturist advised. You see, this friend of mine is one of the gentlest, kindest, most easygoing humans on the planet. But no amount of needles, massages, or chiropractic was going to do for her what she needed to do for herself in order to relieve the discomfort trapped in her body. Healing would come only after she connected to the depths of her rage and expressed it all. Composure was the source of her physical pain. When she called to tell me what her acupuncturist advised her to do, I—probably too quickly—exclaimed, "Yes! Try it!" She laughed and said she was thinking about it.

Optimism: Having cultivated a separate sense of self, Nines in higher levels of awareness are grounded in their bodies, present to themselves and others. Decoupled from their narcotizing routines, they are less concerned with preserving positive, harmonious relationships and experiences and are able to welcome all of reality, including the inevitable conflicts that arise when we show up all the way in our work and our relationships. From this vantage point, Nines are less focused on maintaining the status quo and are able to find genuine optimism in the middle of challenges and conflicts. That's because they have hope that these challenges aren't obstacles to peace but crucibles that will enable richer, more meaningful life experiences.

Stress Management: From Low to High Awareness

Stress is one of the more challenging areas for us to do personal growth work in service to creating healthier emotional intelligence profiles. But the costs of not doing so are high since unaddressed stress will overtake our hearts, bodies, and cognitive functioning, rendering everything else we've been exploring up to this point moot. If we are unable to put stress and anxiety in their proper place, we will suffer greatly (and often make the people around us suffer as well). In today's world, it seems we've almost come to accept high levels of stress as inevitable. Or as a badge of honor. We're fond of telling people how busy we are—that we have too much to do. We do this partly because it's true and partly because (in many cultures) we associate being busy with being successful in a world that is turning faster than ever.

We may have no control over how fast the world spins, but we do have a choice in how fast *we* spin. If we are going to slow the unnecessary rotations in our lives, we must choose to create balance.

I hope it's clear by now that our goal is not to achieve maximum levels of flexibility, tolerance, and optimism in every potentially stressful situation. Each of these attributes may be considered strengths, but any strength can become a liability when overused. As we just learned, for example, Nines are naturally quite flexible as part of their strategy for merging with the opinions, wants, and agendas of others so as to avoid any risk of becoming disconnected from the people they care about. For Nines, then, turning *down* the dial of flexibility may be a tougher yet necessary developmental challenge, whereas for most Eights, turning *up* the volume on flexibility will be precisely what the doctor orders. Sevens often rely too heavily on false optimism, waltzing with their sunny dispositions like they're coaches on *Dancing with the Stars*. They do not need a lesson on how to bring more optimism into their worlds. Most would profit from seeing the whole of reality, including sad and unpleasant things and information that contradicts what they want to believe in order to keep their optimism from being crushed. In contrast, most Sixes I know would benefit from seeing the glass as half full far more than they tend to.

Mitigating chronic stress, as with the rest of our emotional intelligence profiles, is about discovering where we've become chronically dependent on a particular attribute and where we've dismissed other attributes as less important. Integration comes when we can bring these into balance with one another in service to our overall well-being. The path to discovery is made most clear by learning to see which of our personality amplifier settings are turned all the way up to eleven, which ones have been dialed down to almost zero, and why. We don't adjust our settings merely because we know *which* dial we should turn but because we have gained insight as to *why* the settings have been fixed where they are.

As stated previously, by understanding the unconscious motivations and self-limiting beliefs of our dominant type, we gain more optionality and can begin to equip ourselves to readjust our settings like a Nashville music producer, bringing clarity, harmony, and just the right input at the right times. In this way, each part of us—every texture, tone, and instrument—is beautifully expressed with the precision it was designed to achieve. Allowing and/or causing chronic stress in our lives is a distortion pedal on an untuned guitar. It overtakes everything else.

To merely learn to manage stress through various tips, tricks, and hacks is rarely sustainable, as suggested by the epidemic of stress we see in the world. To truly learn to access a healthy balance of flexibility, tolerance, and optimism, we must learn to confront our Ennea-type's egoic attempts to assert control. Everything I've described in the low-awareness sections above are behavioral possibilities (not certainties) when we try to assert control over the outcomes in our lives. Each Ennea-type has particular strategies for asserting control, born out of the loss of trust that they would ever be able to survive without that control. These assertions are the ego's attempt to control consequences, relationships, our sense of security, and even time itself.

So what's the antidote? After all, I'm sure each of us would rather reach and stay in the high-awareness descriptions above. They all seem much more peaceful and true, don't they? But attempting to *will* ourselves to merely think or respond differently to life is futile. We ultimately will not obey our own determination to think differently, relax, handle more, chill out, look on the bright side, or any number of other well-intentioned, half-drunk New Year's Eve resolutions. No matter how committed we are to adopting a different mindset, we ultimately fail in the face of real pressure because we are far too conditioned by the emotional passion of our Ennea-type to ever succeed for long. Willpower is a finite, unsustainable resource in the presence of the passion of our Enneagram type. As stated before, the passion of our type controls us and not the other way around. Part of transcending this vice is to understand that it can never be controlled.

Instead of obedience to such commitments, we need to surrender. We need to lay down the proverbial weapons we've been using to try to "win" at the game of life. To do this, we must first observe all that we can about our coping strategies: the fears and beliefs that drive them, what they did for us, and how they are now hindering us. We must then befriend those stories, thank those stories for any help they gave us in the past, and surrender them. If we don't, we will remain steeped in the stress that comes from attempting to assert the illusion of control. But how do we do it? How do we surrender the passion of our type so we can achieve lasting change? That's the question we'll answer in part 3.

Reflections

1. What are you feeling right now? Say these feelings aloud. Don't move on too quickly. Name them and just let them be.

2. How do your various attempts to control things (situations, people, and outcomes) reveal the fixations of your particular Ennea-type?

3. What wounding message from your childhood is feeding that attempt at control?

4. To what part of your Enneagram type's coping strategies can you now say, "Thank you for helping me with _____ when I needed you," and then release with a whisper, "I no longer need your help with_____"?

PART 3

THE WORK OF TRANSFORMATION

8

Face Your Fear

The cave you fear to enter holds the treasure that you seek.

Joseph Campbell

All personal growth work requires that we face our shadows, those patterns and unhealthy coping mechanisms that can plague us in lower levels of awareness. In doing so, we also have to confront our hidden fears and the false stories we tell about ourselves and the world. Understandably, we avoid these parts of our lives, at least on a conscious level, because they were birthed from uncomfortable experiences and trauma. As I've heard Enneagram master teacher Beatrice Chestnut point out in her CP Enneagram Academy courses, "It causes us pain to face these things about ourselves. Our personality is designed to keep us comfortable."

But when we avoid becoming honest with ourselves because it's too difficult, we end up going where we never wanted to go and living lives we never wanted to live. Avoidance gets us precisely the opposite of what we want, trapping us in patterns that defeat our deepest and most cherished purposes. If we are serious about growing in emotional intelligence, we first must be honest with ourselves, which requires that we open ourselves up to suffering. To walk the map of the Enneagram for the deep transformation it is intended to cultivate, we must let suffering do its work. That may sound masochistic at first, but pain serves a purpose if we have the courage to engage it.

Most of us stop short of this kind of deep encounter. Who isn't afraid of pain? But fear is what keeps us stranded in lower awareness. We don't naturally allow ourselves to realize that many of our default thoughts, feelings, and behaviors are rooted more in fear than desire or rationality as we assume. Each Enneagram type has a dominant fear that keeps us stuck in behavior cycles that run contrary to our truest desires.

Fear is one of our most profound and primal emotions because its main function is to spark our fight-or-flight response in order to keep us alive. Fear is evolutionary wisdom that lives in our blood and our bones, protecting us from the proverbial lion in the Serengeti. In our modern world, however, fear is much more complex. It's no longer as simple as fight-or-flight. The nuances of what we experience now reflect the ways our societies and relationships have grown in complexity. Fears may share the same origin story, but the ways in which they are felt, acknowledged, and expressed are as varied as the societies and cultures in which we live. There are vast differences between the dread of losing our job versus the fear of heights. The panic we feel when we realize we're braking too late and might hit the car ahead is experienced differently than the anxiety that our spouse doesn't love us anymore.

Fears are deeply rooted in our factory settings, stored in muscle memory, passed down in family systems and cultural influences, and fed by painful experiences (both real and perceived). But no matter what kind we experience, fear is always uncomfortable, and we instinctively try to deny, avoid, or quickly overcome it. And that's how we *stay* stuck. Acknowledging our fears is essential for developing awareness.

As I coach my clients in emotional intelligence, I help them un-cover their desires and their fears, which are almost always linked. In fact, I often find that when we think we're moving toward a core desire, in actuality, we are unconsciously moving away from a core fear. For example, someone who stays in a terrible romantic rela-tionship much longer than they should may convince themselves that they *desire* to be with that person when actually they just *fear* being alone. Our minds are hardwired to believe that everything we do is an intentional, positive choice, and yet all the while, fear is often what is running the show. We must excavate and confront these fears. As Carl Jung once said, "Until you make the uncon-scious conscious, it will direct your life and you will call it fate."

If you're still unsure of your dominant Enneagram type, con-sider which of the following fears you most relate to. I've already touched on these fears in the preceding chapters as each type's core motivations and corresponding passion in lower levels of aware-ness are products of fear. However, since much of the work each of us needs to do is found in facing our fears, it is important that we revisit each of these core fears directly so that we can begin to confront the lies they're telling us.

Everyone experiences all nine fears from time to time, but only one core fear *drives* you. It's the fuel that feeds the passion of your type. So as you read the following descriptions, allow yourself to be completely honest. If helpful, ask your trusted friends or team what primary fear they think is calling the shots for you more than others. As you read through these core fears, pay attention to your emotions. Sometimes the thing that most irritates or angers us about other people is the very thing we deny in ourselves.

The Nine Types of Fear

Type One: Fear of being wrong, bad, or corrupted

Ones believe that deep down they are somehow deficient. This fear is less about measuring up to external standards than it is about being right according to their own internal measures. Ones see imperfections everywhere around them and in themselves and strive to live up to impossibly high standards. They never succeed, of course, which is what fuels the passion of *anger.*

Ones don't believe they are motivated by fear at all; they convince themselves that all their ceaseless emphasis on correction is about improving the world. But this is a self-deception. Ones' desire to be perfect is born from the core fear that they aren't good enough, and so they set out to prove to the world—and to themselves—that they are.

Facing your fear: Ones thrive in structured, process-oriented environments, surrounded by competent people, where their own expertise can be expressed and valued. In these settings, it's difficult for them to acknowledge that their core fear is a problem or comes with a cost. But the fear feeds their inner critic, which accuses them of never measuring up to their own ideals or doing enough to change the world. This fear perpetuates a cycle of self-criticism so significant that they become blind to how they are being perceived by others, which is often as being resentful and inflexible.

But fear is a liar. If there's a message I'd like to communicate to Ones, it is this: You *are* good enough. You are *not* deficient. And there are perfections all around you. Even the imperfections are just right in their own way. Facing your fear will enable you to loosen your grip on self-imposed ideals and become more comfortable with gray areas, even while retaining your level of excellence. Appreciating a different perspective and accepting the things you cannot change will create a more relaxed, breathable environment in which mistakes and discovery are welcomed.

Type Two: Fear of being unloved

For Twos, their core fear is felt as a dread of not being needed. If Twos feel unneeded, they believe they are unloved. In organizational settings where tasks are often prioritized over relationships, their emotional needs often go unmet, which only confirms their fear. This can lead them to obsess about the status of important relationships in their lives while neglecting other matters that require attention.

In low awareness, Twos can come across as somewhat manipulative (especially if they are in a prominent role). It can appear as though Twos almost create problems just to solve them and prove to everyone that they are, in fact, *needed*. This strategy is part of what fuels the passion of *pride*.

Facing your fear: Emotions are often not valued as much as they should be—especially at work. This creates a challenging environment for Twos, who long for relational depth with friends and colleagues. But those who behave from a fear of being unneeded risk behaving in ways that will render them unwanted. If you are a Two, the truth is that people aren't thinking about you as often as you are thinking about them. That's not because you are unloved or not needed but because you *are* loved. You *are* needed. Your status in your community is fine and doesn't require overattentiveness to ensure that it stays this way.

Type Three: Fear of worthlessness

Threes are driven by a fear of worthlessness, but they rarely feel this fear because they suppress their own emotions. They work extremely hard to achieve success for themselves and others so that they can demonstrate their worth. Their achievements are often lauded and affirmed time and again, which further convinces Threes that they are motivated by the desire to succeed and not by the fear of failure.

Threes avoid failure at all costs and chase success with reckless abandon—and by all appearances, they are quite successful most of the time. But because their fear is always right below the surface, they are never satisfied with their accomplishments. There's always another mountain to climb or award to win. The biggest risk here is burnout—for themselves and their teams—from a continual pursuit of the next big thing without truly celebrating their achievements or making room for rest. Another cost is that Threes don't generally learn much from failures because their instinct is to deny them and distance themselves from people and projects that won't make them look good.

Facing your fear: The challenge with this core fear is that professional environments reward accomplishment, which makes it hard to recognize its cost. The professionally successful Three rarely experiences a reprieve at home either, as many of their friends and family are cheering them on and sometimes even living through the Three's success. But Threes who let go of the fear that they are worth only what they accomplish are free to focus entirely on creating value in their lives that is harmonious with their authentic desires, freed from the constant pressure of adapting to the values of others.

The fear of worthlessness disconnects Threes from their authenticity, leading them to believe they actually are the role they are playing. This is part of what fuels the passion of *self-deception*. Stress and pressure are the great truth tellers about our core fears. If you're a Three, observe how you respond to these triggers because they reveal if your motives are healthy or if you've identified with others' expectations so much that you are no longer certain of who you are or what you want. This prevents you from experiencing the truth that your heart wants most to know: you are worthy and valuable for just being you—the *real* you.

Type Four: Fear of having no identity of significance

Fours' fear is complex as it is both a fear of not fitting in *and* a fear of being ordinary. Fours feel as if they are on the outside looking in. In the workplace, they may succumb to a feeling of impostor syndrome when in prominent organizational roles. They worry they either don't belong or have sold out their authentic selves by occupying a role that feels too ordinary, too corporate. However, instead of moving past impostor syndrome, they work to be the most unique person in every room, which can get in the way of belonging to the groups they want to be part of.

Fours are often very creative because of their innate drive for the authentic, exceptional, and true. However, underneath it all is a fear of being less-than. This fuels the passion of *envy* and leads to emotional volatility when they're not doing the work of self-acceptance. Because what they communicate can easily change with their emotional tides, which are driven by the fear of being anything other than genuine, their team members and even their intimate relationship partner can often be left feeling confused.

Facing your fear: The cycle this fear produces is a self-fulfilling prophecy. Fours' fixation on discovering their own significant, special identity prevents them from truly being known. This disconnection keeps them obsessing about comparisons and focusing on what is missing instead of recognizing the uniqueness that is already before them.

But here is good news if you are a Four: by confronting this fear and the self-limiting beliefs that come with it, your capacity for human connection is unmatched by any other type on the Enneagram. The deepest truth inside of you is complete contentment and equanimity. Acknowledging and releasing your fear enables you to let go of comparisons, cultivate lasting connections, and receive acceptance and harmony.

Type Five: Fear of incompetence

In some ways, Fives' fear of incompetence is similar to Ones' fear of not being good enough, but for Fives it's all about mental competence. They are afraid of not knowing enough to keep them safe and protected. It is an overreliance on the belief that knowledge is power. They can overvalue those who are cerebral like they are and may too easily dismiss any emotion-driven souls who don't align with how Fives understand the world.

Fives are a withdrawing type, which lets them disconnect from feelings and retreat into the recesses of their minds. They are incredibly analytical as a way of not getting overwhelmed by surprises. What drives this fear is the mindset that there are limits everywhere and that the internal resources they possess—energy, information, affection—are all finite. This mindset fuels the passion of *avarice*. They don't know when they will need these resources, so they hoard them, almost as if preparing for an emotional apocalypse. Because they reserve their energy, Fives come off as standoffish and unavailable, which isn't their intent at all.

Facing your fear: With all their knowledge and understanding, Fives need to intellectualize and process this as well: they will still be able to understand things without hoarding time, space, and energy. They are perhaps the most logical and rational type on the Enneagram, yet more thinking isn't the way to get unstuck. They need to step into their heart center, allowing themselves to fully experience their fear through feeling.

If you are a Five, know that there is a big difference between describing your fear cognitively and experiencing it emotionally. Once you discover that it is possible to allow big feelings in without being consumed by them, you will begin to release your attachments and become more generous with your resources, which is the person you've desired to be all along.

Type Six: Fear of being without support or guidance

All fears are a form of worst-case-scenario thinking, but for Sixes, the fear of being without trustworthy guidance leads them to predict every possible pitfall—and many impossible ones—that *could* happen. They often spiral in a sea of doubts. This leads Sixes to become generally cynical, constantly challenging and questioning the world around them to determine what is trustworthy and what is a safety risk. But instead of moving forward once possible problems are identified, Sixes doubt whether they have made the right decision unless they gather assurance from a trusted authority that everything will be all right, which further fuels the passion of *fear*.

It can be particularly challenging for those who have this core fear to feel the need to face it. After all, worst-case-scenario thinking can actually be helpful when they are surrounded by people who aren't aware of risk or—even more baffling in the eyes of most Sixes—are motivated by risk-taking. Type Six can see around corners that others can't, and that is a good thing. But catastrophizing is exhausting for Sixes and those they lead and live with. This core fear hampers their creativity and precludes the possibility of any blue-sky thinking. It also limits their ability to trust others and themselves, which is the bedrock of any high-performing team.

Facing your fear: Sixes' capability for assessing risks, diagnosing problems, and offering solutions is rooted in their cognitive gifts. However, worst-case-scenario thinking doesn't make people smarter, and worry doesn't add a single day to their lives. In fact, if you identify as a Six, remind yourself that such anxiety is stealing days from you in the long run (but please don't start worrying about that too).

You make good decisions, but the only person who will be able to convince you of that is yourself. Your fear is trying to convince you that you will find certitude about most things, but that simply isn't true. Nothing is certain. But with your natural virtue of courage, you can find peace in the midst of doubt and instability. Practice sitting in the uncertainty, centered in your body, trusting your intuition and your courageous heart.

Type Seven: Fear of being trapped or deprived

The core fear for type Seven is rooted in the belief that if they let sadness or other negative feelings in, they'll be trapped in bleakness forever. These free spirits fear being limited in their options, and this fear compels them to relentlessly pursue fun and new experiences. While they are known for being creative, innovative, and inspiring, it's important for Sevens to realize their constant quest for novelty is an expression of the passion of *gluttony*.

When Sevens are unconscious of their core fear, they relentlessly and sometimes recklessly hunt for opportunity—continually chasing fun and exciting projects. They avoid considering the possible dangers of their actions and underserve or neglect other people's needs. Their fear doesn't allow them to slow down enough to be fully present with people lest their sadness or boredom catches up with them.

Facing your fear: Sevens may be the least likely type on the Enneagram to recognize or acknowledge that they even have a core fear, much less that it is motivating many of their behaviors. But what comes up for them when they seriously consider slowing down and calming their minds is a sense of panic or dread. For Sevens, facing the fear of being trapped requires trapping themselves from time to time, resting from the dizzying pace that keeps them always scanning the horizon for the next source of excitement.

Here's a wise promise if you're a Seven: You do not need to do anything else to feel safe. Instead, you need to stop doing so much. Constant movement and self-distraction can't change reality; they only prevent you from being fully present in reality. You will still be fun and funny, creative and inspiring if you travel at a slower pace. Options will still be available. When you acknowledge your fear of deprivation and release it, you will be free to see and take part in all the stunning freedom available in the here and now.

Type Eight: Fear of becoming vulnerable to control

Eights avoid showing any chinks in their armor so that others are not able to take advantage of them. Driven by their core fear, they seek roles of authority and control in order to avoid being controlled themselves. Their passion is *lust*, which is not necessarily sexual but a lust for enough power to keep themselves safe.

Eights repackage their fear of vulnerability into intensity, anger, and intimidation. Some may aggressively impose their will in order to make it clear who is in charge; however, Eights are often puzzled by the notion that others are intimidated by them. Eights believe they are simply passionate, but this passion can overshadow all other emotions.

Facing your fear: Eights are one of the most misunderstood types on the Enneagram. Their energy can be intense and, yes, intimidating. But it's rooted in a deep commitment to justice and truth, especially when they speak up for those who cannot speak for themselves. Underneath it all, they have one of the most caring and tender hearts of any Enneagram type, which is why they work so hard to proactively defend themselves.

If you are an Eight, know that your vulnerability is not a weakness. Your ability to confidently lead, keep things moving forward, and mentor your team is not dependent upon the degree to which you successfully keep your vulnerability at bay. In fact, your ability to care for others and perform well is actually hampered by this compartmentalization of your authentic self. Facing your fear will augment your ability to successfully bring goodness into the world from a place of warmth instead of the facade of impenetrability. By understanding your fear and releasing it, you will find stronger ground for protecting not only yourself but others as well.

Type Nine: Fear of being separated or in conflict

Those motivated by the fear of conflict are likely to deny their fear's existence or reframe it as a personal value. After all, being a peacemaker is touted as a desirable attribute in a world with countless interpersonal wars. However, there's a sizable difference between peacemaking and peacekeeping. Making peace is an act of the will; it is decisive and strategic. It requires being present in the midst of conflict and leaning in to create relevant and sustainable solutions. Peacekeeping, on the other hand, is the avoidance of conflict. Fear of conflict is what fuels the Nine's passion of *sloth*. They will go to great lengths to preserve the status quo, stuffing down their own opinions and merging with others to prevent any discord.

Facing your fear: Nines do not need to minimize their own importance, silence their opinions, or be lulled into inaction for fear that articulating what they actually want may cause conflict. When they achieve wholeness and integration, they can move from self-denying peacekeepers to fully present peacemakers. The world desperately needs the latter, not the former.

Type Nine is at the center of the Body triad on the Enneagram, which is sometimes called the "anger" triad because anger is often felt as pent-up frustration in the body. Counterintuitive as it might seem, making a conscious choice to fully awaken to the anger welling up inside of them and then expressing that anger will lead Nines to more wholeness and more peace with themselves and others. If you're a Nine and you are worried about the consequences of bringing your anger to the surface, know that you won't stay angry forever. And if you make someone mad, they likely won't be mad at you forever. You are strong and wise enough to handle your biggest emotions and the emotions of others.

Facing Your Fears

Alice: "Where should I go?"
Cheshire Cat: "That depends on where you want to end up."

—Lewis Carroll, *Alice's Adventures in Wonderland*

In their book *The Wisdom of the Enneagram*, Don Richard Riso and Russ Hudson write, "The process of transforming the heart can be difficult because as we open it, we inevitably encounter our own pain and become more aware of the pain of others. In fact, much of our personality is designed to keep us from experiencing this suffering. We close down the sensitivity of our hearts so that we can block our pain and get on with things, but we are never entirely successful in avoiding it."[1]

The truth about facing our fears is that in the short term, doing so is going to cause us suffering. Our core fears are called that because they're at the very root of us, right at the core of our experience. But there's no shortcut to dealing with them, no way to circumvent them. Facing our fears involves suffering, yes, but *not* facing them usually creates even more suffering. As we become aware of the pain our fear is trying to protect against, we are faced with a choice of which type of suffering we are going to experience: the suffering required for waking up and becoming whole, or the suffering required for staying fragmented and asleep.

Before you choose, remember: The body can't lie. If you decide that you don't have to make this choice, that your life is fine the way it is, your body will, over time, tell you whether you are right. My body told me I was wrong while I was driving seventy miles per hour and suddenly couldn't find my breath. And for a long time, I was angry at my body as though it had failed me somehow. But it hadn't; it was serving as a megaphone for a truth I'd been ignoring.

Our brains want to maximize the experience of certainty and minimize surprise. Even when something is unknowable, we'd often rather form an opinion and be wrong than be uncertain. However, the work ahead of us is to step into the uncertainty that comes from dismantling the stories that our core fear has kept us believing all these years. By confronting the lie of our core fears, we have the power to enter a new story. But that story is unwritten, uncertain, and our brains will resist this transformation because, if nothing else, it burns a lot more calories than stasis. However— and I can't stress this enough—believing in the validity of our fears is the biggest thing standing between us and not only mature emotional intelligence but our fullest potential.

We must listen to our bodies and pay attention to our emotions. We must name our sensations, name our feelings, and name our fears—as we are experiencing them. And once we've named the fear, we can question the story we are believing that is giving the fear its power. Questioning our stories helps us learn more about our fears. The more we learn about them, the more conscious of them we become. Self-knowledge is the match that lights the candle of awareness.

From there, we learn to cultivate an inner witness that alerts us when our core fear creeps into our story and pushes us into old unhelpful patterns. A big part of growth work is to simply notice when this happens, conduct a bit of self-inquiry about why it's happening, and then move forward with intention (more on this in the next chapter). This is what my friend Jo did when she truly confronted her fears.

Remember Jo, my Nine friend whose acupuncture story I shared in the previous chapter? She was stuck in the pattern of merging with routines and others as a strategy for keeping her equilibrium. The fear of being cut off from others kept her trapped in self-forgetting, pushing away her own desires and the resentment that it produced. But shortly after her acupuncturist told her that there was nothing more she could do to help her until she released the anger in her body through guttural, unfiltered screams, she decided she would face her fear.

Nines don't identify with their anger because they don't think they are big enough to handle it. Like a Seven who doesn't slow down for fear of being trapped in pain forever, Nines don't allow themselves to directly connect to anger for fear that it will consume them. But my friend soon learned that she was big enough to handle her anger. She drove out to an open field, looked around to make sure she was alone, and screamed until she woke herself up.

Reflections

1. When was the last time you felt fear? Does it reveal anything about your Ennea-type's core fear?

2. Can you think of a time when you confused moving toward a desire with moving away from a fear? What was the result?

3. What personal growth work have you been afraid of starting? What is one small thing you can do today to move you closer to the cave you fear to enter?

9

An Act of Courage

It's never too late to be what you might have been.

George Eliot

Journeying back to our authentic selves and recovering the forgotten essence of who we truly are is an act of courage. We've all so thoroughly forgotten our true selves that to return to our core identity is a journey into the unknown. We cannot be sure of what we'll find when we lay down our defenses. This journey will be filled with possible resistance from those who know our personalities and guaranteed resistance from our personality structures themselves.

A stark reality is that the people in your life may not want you to change. The version of you they've come to know is the one they depend on. For example, if you identify as an Enneagram Two, you are often the first responder of a group—always ready to offer advice or solve a problem. When you begin to understand your compulsion to please as a strategy for feeling liked or wanted, you'll begin combating the urge to overdo and overgive. This is a wise move for you, but don't expect your boundary setting to be universally popular with others; your friends, family members, or coworkers may resist it. They may ask you what's wrong or why you do not seem yourself.

This is true of other types as well; we prefer that people play their usual roles. We want Sevens to continue to be the life of the party, Ones to pursue the excellence they're known for, and Threes to turn on the charm as they perform. When you decide to challenge your default patterns, you may not have much direct support from others. They may not consciously or outwardly battle your growth work, but personal evolution may feel lonely at times, and you may be tempted to return to old habits just to appease the people you care about. This is why growing, healing, and recovering ourselves is an act of courage. It comes with the risk that the people who thought they knew you then may not walk with you now.

If that weren't enough to face, each Ennea-type structure also comes with built-in defenses, which we discussed in chapter 5, that are designed to hold us together and keep our personality strategies intact. Releasing these defenses can be scary since it leads to the very emotions and experiences that we've been avoiding for most of our lives.[1] But there is no waking up, no coming to true awareness, without surrendering the defenses that keep us stuck in our type.

These defenses work automatically on a mostly unconscious level, and they will continue to protect us until we recognize how they are hurting us. Waking up to these habitual patterns takes time. But as Dr. James Hollis writes, "The hero in each of us is required to answer the call of individuation. We must turn away from the cacophony of the outer world to hear the inner voice. When we can dare to live its promptings, then we achieve personhood. We may become strangers to those who thought they knew us, but at least we are no longer strangers to ourselves."[2]

Reaching higher levels of awareness isn't as much about discovering who we need to become as it is about asking ourselves, Who do I need to UN-become if I am to be true to myself? Our personas will fight us on this because they've idealized a self-image and protect us from anything that's a threat to that idealization. That's what our defense strategies are all about. To grow past them, we must intentionally move toward the very thing that we naturally avoid and venture into the unknown. The following table lists the various defense mechanisms of the Ennea-types, the strategies we must forsake if we want to live authentically.

Enneagram Type	Idealized Self-Image	Defense Mechanism Used to Preserve Self-Image
One	"I am right."	Reaction formation
Two	"I am loving."	Repression
Three	"I am a success."	Identification
Four	"I am special."	Introjection
Five	"I am knowledgeable."	Isolation
Six	"I am safe."	Projection
Seven	"I am happy."	Rationalization
Eight	"I am strong."	Denial
Nine	"I am easygoing."	Narcotization

Ennea-Types and Defense Mechanisms

Type One: "I am right."

Ones use the defense of *reaction formation* to avoid anger. Reaction formation is a form of denial that Ones use to convince themselves (and everyone else) that they're not angry. Ones' self-image depends on being good, and their definition of *good* does not include anger or other emotions they view as negative. They idealize a view of themselves as being composed, self-controlled, and above all a force for good. To maintain this self-image, they stuff their anger down and will even go out of their way to do the opposite of whatever they think an angry person would do. For example, if they're frustrated with a son who has not cleaned his room despite being asked multiple times to do so, One parents will do everything they can not to explode. They will make a point of not yelling but will work even harder to keep their cool and ask yet again, possibly with an icy sort of politeness.

Overcoming reaction formation: To begin to surrender your reaction-formation habit, move toward your anger. Get honest about it. Recognize that it is rooted in an ideal of perfection that prevents the experience of serenity in your life. In particular, take notice of when you feel anger in your body—clenching or grinding your teeth, tensing your muscles, or suffering stress-induced gastrointestinal problems. Bodily issues such as these can be your body's way of sending "error" signals to let you know that your experience of life is incongruent with your expectation of it. Your perfectionism prevents you from finding rest and tranquility. Notice your anger, then gently question if it is rooted in truth and righteousness. (Ones always want to believe that it is.) If it is, then take appropriate action, within your sphere of influence, to right the wrongs you see for the sake of justice. If, however, the anger is rooted in perfectionistic idealism, simply notice it, then examine yourself: "What am I believing right now? Is it true? What if what I'm seeing isn't mine to fix?" And perhaps most importantly, "What would I feel if I started to believe that I am already good and there's nothing I need to do to prove it?" Upon accepting the truth that grace is free, all of your striving and straining will naturally dissipate, your body will relax, and your heart will fill with the peace that comes from genuine self-acceptance for exactly who you are right now—nothing more, nothing less.

Type Two: "I am loving."

Twos use the defense of *repression* to avoid their own genuine needs and wants. Repression is hiding one's true feelings and needs from onself and instead focusing on the feelings and needs of others as a way to present a more likable and helpful image. For example, if they feel hurt by an important friend, Twos will do all they can to repress their hurt and instead may become overly nice and flattering to win back the approval of the person who let them down.

Overcoming repression: To cast off your repression habit, you'll have to move toward yourself. Get honest about the ways you try to please and flatter others as a strategy for feeling wanted without asking anyone for anything directly so as to not risk rejection. First, take inventory of your own needs and wants. If you didn't have to take care of other people, what would you most want to be doing? Next—and this is hard for Twos, so take a deep breath beforehand—clearly articulate those desires to the trusted people in your life, even if it means displeasing someone. Notice when you feel a compulsion to divert your attention to the needs and desires of the important people in your life and redirect that attention back to your own feelings and desires. Before doing anything for anyone else, ask yourself, "Is this mine to do?" Remember, always, that your value is not found in winning the approval of others. Your value will be found in simply becoming unapologetically, authentically you.

Type Three: "I am a success."

Threes use the defense of *identification* to avoid failure and maintain an image of success. Identification is taking on a particular role or expectation so completely that one loses all sense of who they really are. For example, not wanting to acknowledge or admit any doubts or personal struggles, a Three pastor avoids honest conversations with trusted friends. Instead, they try even harder to impress people with their gift of gab until the bottom falls out and they suffer a stress-related health issue and/or great moral failure.

Overcoming identification: If you are a Three, you may find the abdication of your defense mechanism particularly difficult because you get so much approval when you obey its mandate for success, and approval has always been the name of the game for you. It follows, then, that giving up your identification habit means moving toward your failures. Acknowledge them. Get honest about the things you are doing each day that serve to project an idealized image at the expense of your heart's true desires. Feel what it's like to connect with someone on a deeply personal level without contemplating their utility in your life. Pay full attention to their emotions and allow the full spectrum of your own feelings to surface, be experienced, and be communicated. Turn down the volume on the cheering and applauding that push you toward perpetual adaptation, and ask yourself, "Who would I be if I believed I could be just as loved, just as revered, and just as successful for being me and only me every day—nothing more, nothing less?"

Type Four: "I am special."

Fours use the defense of *introjection* to avoid feeling deficient or ordinary and to present an image of being authentic. Introjection is the unconscious adoption of the ideas or attitudes of others in both positive and negative ways. For example, a Four wanting to compensate for a painful feeling of lack may introject and romanticize a past relationship and, simultaneously, shoulder the entire blame for why the relationship ended as subconscious evidence for their feelings of personal deficiency.

Overcoming introjection: To quit your unhealthy pattern of introjection, move toward the ordinary. Get honest about your tendency to idealize people, places, and experiences as an attempt to mask painful feelings of lack. Notice all the times you overidentify with suffering as a way to feel special. Start saying three things out loud each day that you are grateful for as a way to become more anchored in the present and to challenge the false story you carry that something is missing. Take inventory of all you have and acknowledge that this present moment is all there is. Ask yourself, "What would my life feel like if I believed the truth that I am whole and complete, not lacking anything? Who would I be if I no longer feared being ordinary? How would I feel if I truly believed that I am wonderfully made?"

Type Five: "I am knowledgeable."

Fives use the defense of *isolation* to avoid depletion. Isolation is a withdrawing from others and one's own emotional experience; it's to substitute presence with knowledge. For example, you share some upsetting medical news with your Five friend, and rather than sitting in the sadness and being emotionally present to you, they immediately begin calculating potential causes and solutions and sharing all they know about what you can do.

Overcoming isolation: To surrender your isolation habit, move toward your heart. Allow yourself to fully *feel* your emotions instead of just thinking about them. By opening up your heart center you will become more available to others as you learn to experience each moment and share all that you have willingly and freely. Notice that you're able to do this without becoming overwhelmed. When you withdraw into your head, you invite the very intrusions from others that you fear since they want to get inside and be near to you. However, when you become fully present to others, they no longer need to come looking for you; you're already there. Reassure yourself daily, "My life is filled with abundance. I don't need to hold on to anything. The tides come in, and the tides go out. And I can be present in this moment because I have all that I need."

Type Six: "I am safe."

Sixes use the defense of *projection* to ascribe to others what they cannot accept in themselves. Projection is a way of outsourcing emotions to relationships or authority figures in order to feel safe or justify their distrust. For example, a Six, wanting to combat a feeling of generalized anxiety and present an image of loyalty, may dogmatically subscribe to a particular political figure or ideology. Once committed, they may exclude any information that would suggest that this particular authority figure or belief system isn't necessarily worthy of their allegiance. In the same way, they may project feelings of distrust onto any person, system, or group that threatens their sense of safety and certainty.

Overcoming projection: To relinquish your defense mechanism of projection, move toward your fear of being rejected and without enough support. Your self-limiting and untrue belief that you don't have enough guidance leads to overly positive *and* overly negative projections onto various relationships and authority figures as a way to justify your internal angst and to deny self-doubt. But doubt is not the enemy of faith; certainty is. Every time you think, question, and try to build alliances as an attempt to reach mental certainty, you push yourself further away from the courageous faith you naturally possessed before it was trounced somewhere in your childhood story. However, when you accept that the world will always be uncertain, you can begin to release your attempts to control the outcomes and reclaim your trust and faith that all will unfold as it is meant to. Tell yourself as often as necessary, "I am bigger than my fear. I do not need to trade away my power to feel safe. Some questions are unanswerable, and that's okay. It's not my job to answer them."

Type Seven: "I am happy."

Sevens use the defense of *rationalization* to avoid suffering. Rationalization is a way of reframing negatives into positives for oneself and others while justifying one's own, sometimes impulsive, behaviors. For example, a Seven parent whose child has just suffered a trauma may fast-forward past their experience and immediately start focusing on all the good that can surely come from it—ways in which it will bring the family closer, and so on. If confronted by their spouse about their inappropriate response, they may rationalize their comments as simply making lemonade out of lemons or trying to cheer the child up.

Overcoming rationalization: When you commit to abandoning your rationalization habit, move toward the sad and difficult things in your life without reframing them or looking for the bright side. It's perfectly okay if there aren't any bright sides. If people in your life are going through hard things, practice just sitting with them in an empathetic and compassionate posture, being fully present. Don't speak; just listen without contemplating new possibilities for you or them. Notice that you're able to be there for as long as necessary, and you won't ever be stuck there. Understand that suffering is unavoidable. It comes, and it always leaves again. If suffering is not allowed to visit and the mind tries to escape through planning and other mental gymnastics, the body will hold it and hold it until one day it can't be contained any longer. The consequences of that could be catastrophic. Remind yourself every day, "I may always have impulses, but I needn't act on them. It is safe for me to slow down and deny my appetite for stimulation. I won't find personal gratification in excess but in the inner calm that comes with being present in my own experiences and to the ones I love."

Type Eight: "I am strong."

Eights use the defense of *denial* to avoid vulnerability. Denial is a way of negating thoughts, feelings, and data that are contrary to what one wants or that makes one feel weak or exposed in some way. For example, sensing that a team member is going to deliver unpleasant realities about the status of a project, the Eight boss may power up and reject the news before they've even heard it, doubling down on what it is they're after and demanding that everyone do what they have to in order to get things done.

Overcoming denial: If you want to discard your denial habit, move toward your feelings. Embrace a more tender emotional experience without trying to power through uncomfortable feelings. Get honest about your penchant for controlling your environment—rather than simply being in it—for fear that someone may exert control over you if you don't get the upper hand. Open your heart and mind to others, creating safety and space for divergent views, and actively embrace someone else's idea as preferential to your own when the opportunity arises. Pay attention to the ways in which you create intensity around you and then intentionally start turning down the volume. Notice the peace that comes from connecting to your heart and your mind and the greater freedom you feel when you are receptive to others. Remember the end goals and tell yourself, "My life will be fuller when I allow and embrace the full breadth of my emotional experience instead of denying it. Overpowering others isn't a strength but a sign of fear. If I want to be seen as strong, I will be vulnerable."

Type Nine: "I am easygoing."

Nines use the defense of *narcotization* to avoid internal and external conflict. Narcotization is a way of numbing experiences that seem too big, uncomfortable, painful, or challenging. For example, a Nine employee who is unhappy at their job may engage in comfortable routines, eating, drinking, watching TV, exercising, or any other activity requiring little thought or energy to avoid what feels like an overwhelming process of putting their résumé together, looking for jobs, and going on interviews.

Overcoming narcotization: As you opt out of narcotization, move toward the things that will disrupt your internal and external experiences. You *want* some disharmony and conflict. Get honest about all the habitual routines that keep you asleep to yourself, even ones that seem positive such as compulsively going to the gym. Connect to your anger and reclaim your voice. Speak a contrary point of view and notice how others appreciate you showing up all the way. Even when conflict ensues, observe how much more awake and honest you feel for having taken a stand. Take inventory multiple times a day of what you are feeling and desiring. When your routines threaten to interfere with acting on your true desires, it's time to break those routines again. Ask yourself, "What would my life look like if I loved myself as much as I show love to others? What will I commit to accomplishing today that will move me tangibly closer to my goals?"

Laying Down Your Defenses

Surrendering our defenses is an ongoing process of noticing them and then releasing them. However, learning to notice when you've stopped noticing is the most difficult work of all. Losing self-awareness, by definition, means you won't recognize when you've lost it. We need mechanisms that keep us connected to ourselves—friends and community who support our growth, openness to feedback, proactive self-inquiry, and daily practices (such as those suggested in the final chapter of this book)—to ensure that we are staying self-aware.

As professor of philosophy and theologian Dallas Willard says, "Familiarity breeds unfamiliarity."[3] The longer we identify with the passion of our Ennea-type, the less familiar our truest selves become to us. The longer we live on autopilot, the more foreign our virtue becomes to us. Our defense mechanisms may be harming us, but at least they are the devil we know. Like one who is abused willfully returning to their abuser, we are tempted to choose the mask—the known quantity—over the arduous voyage to freedom. Familiarity is the enemy of growth.

If transformation is what we desire, we must refuse to satiate ourselves with our familiar habits and distractions. Transformation happens in the presence of truth, and the truth is that we need to actively start paying attention to what we are paying attention to. To do that, we must break our addiction to the habitual distractions that remove discretionary reflection time from our lives and keep us comfortably self-forgetting. When we self-remember, we can then start to self-reflect on the ways in which our programmed behaviors have been hindering us. By reflecting often enough, we then develop the skill to self-observe.

Self-Remembrance→Self-Reflection→Self-Observation

Self-observation is self-reflection happening in real time. We learn to see ourselves as if we are an objective witness observing from a distance. We are then able to choose consciously, in the moment, a course of action that is informed, without assumption, and unmotivated by fears, anger, or image. For example, a Six who has spent regular time reflecting on the ways in which they've allowed fear to control their decisions will learn to hear that fear whispering in their ear in real time. They are then able to stop and say, "Gosh, I guess I don't really need all ten cases of Costco toilet paper right now."

When we self-observe, we are fully present to ourselves in the moment. But this growth work isn't a decisive one-time endeavor. It is a daily choice—a choice to direct our attention where it needs to go.

One of my clients who leads with type Nine learned to recognize her defense mechanism of narcotization when she realized that over a period of more than three years, she hadn't taken any tangible steps toward the career goals she professed to have. After remembering *why* she aspired for the job she hadn't tried to get, she was able to reflect on all the distracting behaviors that kept her comfortable at the expense of pursuing her dreams with vigor. After committing to doing her personal growth work, she is better able to see when the stress of going after what she wants in life tempts her to lose herself in a reality TV show (or some other mindless activity) instead. She now has the capacity to stop and ask herself, "Is what I want *now* the thing I want *most*?" For her, the answer is almost always no.

In short, self-awareness flows from self-remembrance. There is no self-awareness while we remain asleep to ourselves. Until we do the work of self-remembrance, we are emotionally conditioned, mentally distracted, and physically functioning out of habit most of the time. This way of operating feels normal to us, even when it isn't working to get us what we want. One of the biggest barriers to our personal evolution is believing that our usual way of seeing, feeling, and behaving is normal. But as I hope you can appreciate after having read a bit about the primary Ennea-types, there is no *normal*, only familiar. And familiarity opposes our growth.

Reflections

1. What reflection practices can you begin today that will help you to become self-remembering and self-aware?

2. Think of someone in your life who would make a trusted accountability partner for the personal growth commitments you are making. Schedule a time to speak with that person and specifically ask them to help you.

3. What is a specific way you can begin to move toward the very thing your defense mechanism has previously prevented you from confronting?

10

Practices for the Path Forward

To contact the deeper truth of who we are, we must engage in some activity or practice that questions what we assume to be true about ourselves.

A. H. Almaas

In this book, we've looked at five measures of emotional intelligence through the lens of the Enneagram. We've explored what low and high awareness might look like for each type. We've also discussed the core fears and defense mechanisms that work together to keep us stuck in our emotional vices, unable to transcend our self-limiting beliefs and false narratives until we do the difficult, ongoing work of waking up.

This chapter offers some final thoughts on how to do that work—specifically, how to use the Enneagram as a tool to help us wake up and reclaim our true selves. We'll explore what the Enneagram has to teach us about the integration of all three centers of intelligence—Head, Body, and Heart. We'll also delve into how to use the Enneagram's wings and arrows as resources to help us create more balance in our lives so that our core Ennea-type doesn't preclude us from other ways of seeing the world. We'll investigate how the Enneagram's passions correlate to Christianity's traditional seven deadly sins and how learning more about our type's leanings toward one (or more) of these areas can cause us and others pain. Finally, we'll take a look at ways we can be more compassionate to people of all types, recognizing that, for example, the kind of relationship a Five wants is going to be very different from what a Two wants. The tools and practices we use to grow beyond the limitations of our personality type aren't just for our own benefit; they are also a gift to others and are meant to be shared.

Uniting the Heart, Head, and Body

Any practice that aims to get us unstuck has to start somewhere, and here is my main suggestion for what you need to do to move toward transformation:

Slow down.

Slow. Down.

S-l-o-w . . . d-o-w-n . . . the automation in your life. I know this isn't the first time I've given this piece of advice in the book, but that's because it's consistently true and bears repeating. Whether you're a future-focused, highly active type running from one thing to another or you're too busy binge-watching Netflix to focus on what matters most to you, the first step toward self-remembrance is to slow down the *automation* and notice where habits are running you. We cannot begin to self-reflect and self-observe, let alone evolve, if we do not slow our automated, conditioned behaviors. When you create enough space to breathe and to observe, you're ready to think about integrating your three centers of intelligence.

For the Heart

We simply cannot access the heart while rushing through life and always up in the mind or satiating the body, frequently distracted by electronic devices or physical pleasures. Engaging the heart means putting down the phone. It means sitting in the silence and *feeling* our feelings. We must learn to do this not as an indulgence but as an accelerant for change. We must learn to experience and name both the comfortable and the painful emotions so that we can hear what our heart is telling us and learn to distinguish the conditioned from the unconditioned emotions in each of us.

Earlier, we saw that there are no good or bad emotions: some emotions are positively felt and others are negatively felt, but all are data. Building on this concept, let's turn to the teachings of George Gurdjieff, a Russian philosopher whose pioneering ideas about Head types, Heart types, and Body types would influence the development of the modern Enneagram. Gurdjieff taught that the only truly negative emotions are the ones that are conditioned in us[1]—in other words, the emotions that are simply the by-product of living unconsciously in low levels of awareness. Continually paying attention to what we are feeling is of critical importance. Distinguishing between what is an unconditioned emotion meant to give us new insights and what is an automatic feeling associated with the emotional vice of our Enneagram type is an important step toward the kind of emotional agility that accelerates our personal evolution.

For example, a Four who learns to recognize that their frequent emotional experience of sadness is a largely conditioned experience, rooted in a false belief about who they are and their place in the world, can learn to question that feeling and the story behind it. If, on the other hand, they don't recognize that the sadness that frequently creeps in is rooted in a broken narrative, they'll experience the emotion solely as confirmation that they don't belong or are deficient in some way. Conditioned emotional responses work to keep us trapped in an automated Think→Feel→Act behavior cycle that prevents us from growing beyond the limitations of our Ennea-type structure and toward conscious, healthy, emotionally intelligent living. The more committed growth work that we do, the better we will become at depicting conditioned versus unconditioned emotions.

Your heart is asking for a bit of your time each day to engage with your head. It longs to be fully experienced. It has invaluable things it wants to share with you. Create the space for it.

For the Head

A daily mindfulness practice—whether self-directed or directed through an app or personal guide—is crucial to learning how to focus our attention. Just as we have feelings that are conditioned by the emotional vice of our Ennea-type, we have an automatic focus of attention that serves to reinforce our type's belief systems. The move from vice to virtue necessitates that we learn how to take back control of what we pay attention to. Mindfulness work helps to train our brains to learn to pay attention to what needs our attention.

Some Ennea-types may have an easier time with this than others, but like any form of exercise, everyone has the capacity for developing this muscle. The key to success is patience and self-compassion. Your mind will inevitably drift to the future and to the past when you practice mindfulness. Simply notice when this happens and gently bring yourself back to your breath. This breath, then the next breath. Each inhale and each exhale are the only present moments there are. Gently teach yourself to be here, now, by always coming back to your breath.

Start off slowly if you're new to this practice—perhaps just three minutes per day. Then try four minutes, and so on. Graduating to just ten minutes per day will positively connect your heart, mind, and body, reduce stress, increase clarity, and help you get centered in your body. The harder you find this practice to be, the more you need to be disciplined about doing it.

When you're not doing mindfulness work, keep feeding your brain with new insights about your Ennea-type and the types of those with whom you live and work. Consider attending an Enneagram workshop or intensive training led by reputable, expert teachers. We can't change what we don't know, so commit to your learning. Ongoing study is important.

For the Body

Practice listening to your body instead of merely trying to control it. Our bodies store a wealth of information and communicate to us through the senses. It is imperative that we listen. When is your body signaling that it is fearful? When is it communicating safety? When is it warning you that your brain's predictions about something are incorrect? What else is it trying to tell you?

As part of your mindfulness practice, incorporate a body scan. Body scanning involves sitting or lying down, then slowly directing attention to each part of your body, starting with the top of your head and gradually moving down to your face, neck, chest, arms, abdomen, back, legs, and feet, giving each body part adequate time to speak to you. Notice any tension or aches that you may perceive in any one of these areas. Simply observe that tension, then try to breathe into it and give your body permission to release it. Practice this body scan daily, and register what it is doing for your head and your heart over time.

I was recently shown an effective way to connect to what is going on in my body by using a pulsometer. Simply put the pulsometer on your index finger and set a timer for one minute. Before starting the timer, take some deep, cleansing breaths and tune in to your heartbeat. Then start the timer. Count every heartbeat for one minute and write down the total number of beats that you counted. Then look at the pulsometer to see how many beats per minute it recorded. The difference between those two numbers will tell you a bit about how attuned you are to what is going on in your body. Try it every day until there is consistently almost no difference between the two numbers. When you're able to develop that level of bodily awareness, you'll start to become more attuned to what else is going on in your body and the messages it is sending you. This allows the mind and the body to become more in sync.

Finally, get into your body with a committed exercise routine. Exercise is one of the most overlooked aspects of developing our awareness, but it's vital to our growth work. Not only is the body designed for movement, but the brain is as well. Your mental clarity will significantly improve through regular exercise.[2] I'm not talking about any particular form of exercise, though different movements have different brain benefits, nor am I talking about any particular fitness goal. We all need a way to get into our bodies. If we neglect the body, the brain and the heart suffer as well (literally and figuratively). Find a practice that works for you and to which you can commit.

Whichever practices you choose, your body is asking permission to invert the pattern of top-down communication from your brain to your limbs and to do some of the thinking and communicating for a change. Practice letting it.

Integration

Regardless of your Ennea-type, each of us must engage in consistent practices if we want to grow. To better understand your broken story, to process any trauma, or to learn techniques for developing greater awareness, please consider finding a qualified therapist whom you trust.

Commit to your mindfulness practice. Get a massage and focus only on the massage. Consider taking up yoga. Yoga is an effective way to learn to link our breath with our movement. According to a local yoga instructor I spoke to, when practicing yoga regularly, your body will start to learn how to connect breath to movement in everyday life, which helps to calm your nervous system and to become more cognizant of a disconnect between your mind and body.

More than anything, prioritize the most important form of renewal there is: getting good sleep. The focus of this book has been on learning how to wake up from our semiconscious, automatic, reactive lives. But every single suggestion I've made for getting there is predicated on practices of physical, mental, emotional, and spiritual renewal—none of which are possible if we aren't getting consistent and deep sleep. Sleep is essential to us being able to manage our inner resources. So commit to a specific bedtime and stick with it. Put down your phone and tablet a couple of hours before bed, curb your post-dinner snacks or drinks, and then see what happens. I am confident that you'll find regular, restful sleep will do wonders for your awareness.

Above all, embrace self-compassion. You will have ups and downs, small wins, and mistakes. And that's okay. It's expected. It is all part of the process. Just don't give up on yourself!

When we integrate all three intelligence centers through intentional practices, the Think→Feel→Act cycle begins to come undone. Instead of being limited by a flow of energy from the head through the heart to the body, we now learn to also consciously perceive reality from the body through the heart to the head. We become connected to our sensory perceptions in an embodied way, and we begin to see the distinction between our conditioned and unconditioned emotions. In essence, we are able to access all three intelligence centers as appropriate. This widens the space between stimulus and response and gives us back our choices, our freedom.

Using Your Enneagram Wings and Arrows to Create Balance

We each have two Enneagram wings. They are the numbers to the immediate left and right of our dominant Ennea-type. Our

Enneagram wings are there to provide balance and assist us along our growth paths. When we overidentify with one wing, we are communicating where we feel most stuck. For example, someone who says "I'm a Three wing Four" is messaging that they naturally identify with more elements of type Four than they do with type Two. What this points to is that they have work to do in bringing up their Two wing.

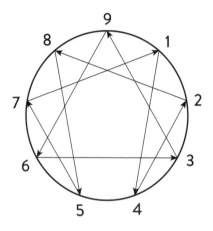

When we have equal access to both our wings, we begin to feel sturdier—more balanced. After spending a considerable amount of time creating balance across both of our wings, we can begin to access and work with our arrows for additional growth and support.

While much Enneagram theory teaches where we unconsciously tend to move in both stress (to the number on the arrow that points *away* from our dominant type) and security (to the number on the arrow that points *toward* our dominant type), the arrows (like our wings) are primarily there as resources, pointing us to the growth work that can help us transcend the limitations of our dominant type.

Stretch yourself with the use of your wings and arrows. For each type, use your wings to create balance. With your wings intact, walk the arrows to create even more balance.

Type One

Wings: Nine and Two

Arrows: Seven and Four

Goal: To be spontaneous. To do less. To allow mistakes to happen. To choose fun over duty.

Nine Wing: Leverage this wing to help you become more adaptable. Leaning on this wing will support you in having more compassion toward yourself and others since Nines are one of the most accepting types on the Enneagram. A Nine wing will also help you see that there is more than one right perspective and that you are not required to fix everything all the time.

Two Wing: Leverage this wing to help you connect with other people's feelings. This wing will support you in building and maintaining important relationships and give you more sensitivity to the needs around you. When Ones draw on their Two wing, they give freely of their time and energy in the service of others.

Seven Arrow: Explore options for doing some things differently at point Seven. Integrate lightness, fun, and humor into how you show up. Sevens are natural risk-takers, and a dose of their energy can help you see the joy of trying new ventures, even if you don't do them perfectly.

Four Arrow: Now that you're more open to new possibilities, incorporate a focus on creativity and meaning at point Four in order to balance your natural attention on processes and tasks. Fours are capable of dreaming big! From Four you can also learn to mine your own feelings, even the unpleasant ones you tend to suppress, finding the wisdom in anger, sadness, or pain.

Type Two

Wings: One and Three

Arrows: Four and Eight

Goal: To learn to say no. To become deeply connected to your own desires. To curb flattery from others.

One Wing: Leverage this wing to help you pay more attention to procedures and tasks. Leaning on this wing will support you in staying balanced, measured, and consistent. A One wing will help you achieve your goals with less concern about your relationship status or image.

Three Wing: Utilize this wing to help you be more productive. Leveraging this wing will support you in valuing your own contributions since Threes are proud of their accomplishments. When Twos draw on their Three wing, they learn to see around corners and paint a picture of success for themselves and others.

Four Arrow: Connect to your own wants and feelings at point Four. Allow your attention to be directed inward in order to bring balance to your natural outward focus on others. From accessing your emotions at point Four, you become more open to new possibilities and increase your focus on creativity and personal meaning.

Eight Arrow: Once you connect to your own feelings and needs, be direct about them by integrating the assertiveness found at point Eight. From Eight, you can ask for what you need head-on and without pretense. Here you find your power without needing approval.

Type Three

Wings: Two and Four

Arrows: Six and Nine

Goal: To slow down and connect with feelings. To allow people and processes to operate in their own time without forcing anything. To no longer confuse identity with accomplishment.

Two Wing: Leverage this wing to help you build relationships, focusing on the feelings of others with genuine empathy and concern. This wing will give you more sensitivity to the needs around you. When Threes lean on their Two wing, they connect with others from the heart and without contemplating the utility of the person they are with.

Four Wing: A Four wing can help you understand and express your own emotions, even the painful ones. Leaning on this wing will support you in cultivating deeper, authentic meaning in your life, help you slow down, and give you access to your genuine values and desires.

Six Arrow: Now that you're more connected to your own emotions and the needs of others, take time to question your plans at point Six. Ask questions about what could go wrong before getting into action as a way to be more methodical and expose potential risks. Point Six can help you own your mistakes as learning opportunities rather than distancing yourself from failure.

Nine Arrow: Upon integrating this slower approach, start genuinely listening to others' viewpoints at point Nine, considering all feelings and opinions equally. From Nine, you can learn to be patient, hold eye contact, and make selfless decisions that are truly in the best interest of others.

Type Four

Wings: Three and Five

Arrows: One and Two

Goal: To rely on thoughts and actions as much as feelings. To allow emotions to come and go without overidentifying with any one in particular. To release the grip on suffering.

Three Wing: Employ this wing to help you focus on important goals and related tasks. A Three wing will support you in shifting your attention from inward to outward, enabling you to metabolize your feelings more quickly, so that you may deliver on your commitments. When Fours lean on their Three wing, they get into action more quickly and focus on results.

Five Wing: Call upon this wing to help you analyze your emotions to make sense of the information they are giving you. A Five wing offers you a thoughtful objectivity that can help you observe your feelings from more of a distance. When Fours lean on their Five wing, they get more cerebral and find as much value in careful analysis as they do their emotional experience.

One Arrow: Now that you're better connected to thinking and doing, direct your focus toward tasks and quality at point One. From One, learn to appreciate the importance of details and mundane activities that ensure consistent and good results. Point One will help you to stay balanced, measured, and consistent.

Two Arrow: Release your grip on your own emotional experience by directing your attention toward others at point Two, leading to a healthier balance between the inward and outward experience of emotion. At point Two, you're better able to serve others and impact the world in meaningful and tangible ways.

Type Five

Wings: Four and Six

Arrows: Eight and Seven

Goal: To get out of the head and into the body. To be less hesitant and take decisive action. To allow the full experience of life to affect you.

Four Wing: Exercise this wing to help you expand your capacity for real-time emotional experience. Leaning on this wing will support you in connecting to the wisdom of the heart. Fours have more access to their feelings than any other Ennea-type, so leveraging this wing will expand your thinking through contact with emotions.

Six Wing: Let this wing bring to light any denied fear inside you. A Six wing will help you recognize when your proclivity toward analysis is merely an avoidance tactic for acting on something that scares you. Allow the Six wing to remind you of the trusted people in your life whom you can depend on to help you get unstuck.

Eight Arrow: Now that you're better connected to your emotions, learn to own your power and decisiveness at point Eight. Allow yourself to feel things passionately, and express yourself without hesitation or overthinking. Point Eight offers you the power to go after what you want without fear of becoming depleted.

Seven Arrow: Upon integrating your decisiveness and power at point Eight, cast your eye outside yourself at point Seven. Expand your experience through some lightness, fun, and pleasure seeking. Sevens are natural risk-takers, and a dose of their energy can help you see the joy of trying new things, even if you don't have all the information.

Type Six

Wings: Five and Seven

Arrows: Nine and Three

Goal: To trust yourself. To accept uncertainty. To take some risks. To stop trying to control the outcome.

Five Wing: This wing can mitigate your fear with research. Taking advantage of this wing will offer you added assurance that you're well informed of potential risks and can do what is necessary to appropriately mitigate them without the need for further questioning.

Seven Wing: Leaning on the Seven wing will help you jump into action even when you aren't sure what will happen. Leveraging this wing will support you in getting comfortable with spontaneity, helping you see all the possibilities instead of pitfalls. Seven's energy will keep you moving forward.

Nine Arrow: With more access to information from your Five wing and more openness and spontaneity with your Seven wing, allow relaxation and the release of worry at point Nine. This will help you to get out of your head and into your body, just going with the flow of the group without poking holes in their plans. Point Nine will also help you see that there is more than one right perspective and that you are not required to fix everything all the time.

Three Arrow: Upon learning to go with the flow at point Nine, begin to move forward toward your goals with a focus on progress at point Three. Learn to cut an unimportant corner or two on your way to the finish line as Three teaches you to shift your attention from risks to results.

Type Seven

Wings: Six and Eight

Arrows: Five and One

Goal: To accept limitations as a source of meaning. To intentionally decline certain invitations. To refrain from acting on all of your ideas. To allow for a bit of stillness and boredom.

Six Wing: Leverage this wing to help you face and accept negative realities. A Six wing will strengthen your ability to slow down and take an honest look at what might not be working. Leaning on this wing will empower you to thoughtfully question your plans and limit impulsivity.

Eight Wing: Draw on this wing to help you shift your focus from plans to results. An Eight wing provides Sevens with a decisiveness that can counterbalance your natural inclination to jump from one thing to the next. Wing Eight has the power to straighten your path and give you the clarity and energy to keep your eyes on the prize.

Five Arrow: Now that you're seeing more, excluding less, and feeling more focused, direct your attention inward at point Five. Spend time alone in healthy reflection and analysis, allowing your concerns to rise to the surface and learning to just be with them. Stillness is a gift of the Five that can help you find the rest you need.

One Arrow: From a slower, more introspective posture, learn to embrace structure, process, and limitations at point One. Notice that rules can enable your visions to become sustainable realities instead of merely fleeting ideas. One will give you the appreciation for seeing to the details of plans and projects and finding fulfillment in following through from start to finish.

Type Eight

Wings: Seven and Nine

Arrows: Two and Five

Goal: To see vulnerability for the strength that it is. To turn down the volume on the intensity of your presence. To connect with and show tender emotions. To think and feel before doing.

Seven Wing: Turn to this wing to help you lighten up and be more playful. Leaning on this wing will support you in becoming less determined about your present course of action as you learn to open up and consider more possibilities. This wing has the potential to soften your intensity with joy.

Nine Wing: Leverage this wing to help you listen to and care for others with tenderness. From the Nine wing, learn to consider diverse perspectives without forcing your own will or agenda on the group. This wing offers you rest, rejuvenation, and the ability to just go with the flow of life.

Two Arrow: From a lighter and more open place, now allow yourself to soften and connect with others at point Two. Point Two will give you a better sense of what others want and need from you. Share more of who you are, including your vulnerabilities, without fear. Allow Two to teach you to serve people and give you an appropriate amount of awareness of how you are being received by others.

Five Arrow: After integrating the heart at point Two, move into your head and give yourself adequate time for contemplation at point Five. Point Five will help you to think and analyze before taking any action. Five offers the gift of stillness that will enable you to self-reflect and make measured, thoughtful decisions.

Type Nine

Wings: Eight and One

Arrows: Three and Six

Goal: To connect deeply with your own desires and take daily, decisive action on your goals. To speak up without fear of conflict. To make your presence felt and own your anger.

Eight Wing: Utilize this wing to connect to your confidence and discover any appropriate anger you may be feeling. This wing will give you the audacity to voice your concerns without fear of conflict or disturbing your inner sense of peace. Leveraging this wing has the power to propel you from inertia to action.

One Wing: With a One wing, you can prioritize your plans and organize the process it will take to achieve them. Leaning on this wing will support you in meeting your goals with precision and timeliness. While your Eight wing gives you the resources for action, leaning on your One wing will move you into *right* action. Ones are one of the most dutiful types there are, so leaning on this wing will support you in staying balanced, measured, and consistent.

Three Arrow: From a place of energized consistency, step onto center stage at point Three. Point Three will show you that your opinions and contributions are valuable. Connect to your vision and take decisive action on your own behalf, believing in and embracing your own success. Point Three gives you a voice to define and reach your goals.

Six Arrow: After integrating decisiveness and confidence at point Three, allow yourself to embody the contrarian voice at point Six. Speak up and question those you doubt or disagree with. Also, point Six can imbue you with a collective strength; Sixes are about furthering the success of the team, not just the individual.

The preceding growth work suggestions can be practiced alone, but it is highly advantageous to start doing this work with a qualified Enneagram teacher or coach. These practices cannot be rushed; they aren't items to tick on your to-do list. They require patience, guidance, and support. Consider finding a community of committed individuals who are also doing this work. Our trusted, interpersonal relationships are so beneficial to our evolution.

Doing Your Spiritual Work

The growth work we've been looking at is both psychological and spiritual in nature. The latter is often dependent upon a healthy respect and approach to the former. Attempting to sidestep healthy psychological work (often with a therapist, coach, or counselor) in favor of the transcendent is known as *spiritual bypassing*. That term was coined by psychotherapist John Welwood, and he described it as the "tendency to use spiritual ideas and practices to sidestep or avoid facing unresolved emotional issues, psychological wounds, and unfinished developmental tasks."[3]

A Seven who reframes all their hardships as blessings from God is an example of spiritual bypassing. Another example is a Four who avoids confronting the wounding message from their childhood story that keeps them believing they are deficient somehow and instead attempts to transcend their pain by jumping headfirst into a new spiritual practice they are convinced, in the moment, will make them feel whole again. This is not said to evaluate or in any way criticize spiritual practices or to question if a hardship may or may not be a gift from God. The point is that it's tempting to try to jump to the vertical at the expense of the horizontal, meaning we substitute the work we must do by trying to catapult ourselves to a place where the pain cannot find us. But those spiritual experiences tend to be temporary, as the weight of unaddressed wounds and traumas has a habit of pulling us back down. Like seeds that fall on rocky ground, spiritual experiences will wither in the shallow soil of our unaddressed wounds.

It's a false dichotomy to think we must choose between two parts of the whole. Our spiritual experiences are enhanced by the healing that comes from psychological work. And our psychological work can benefit exponentially from healthy spiritual practices. We need both. The work that lies ahead for each of us on a growth path involves layers of somatic, psychological, and spiritual elements if we are to move beyond our emotional vices and recover our emotional virtues.

Whatever your spiritual tradition and practices, incorporate them with intentionality into your growth work. God beckons us to surrender, to deny ourselves. In my view, these words are directed straight to the ego—the false self—which is precisely the part of us that interferes with being able to hear the divine whisper or experience the transcendent. It is the armor we wear to stop the bullets from getting through. But that armor is often so successful that in the process, it also blocks our access to the love, warmth, and fullness of what it is to be wholly human, without armor, walking in courage and faith.

In the Christian tradition, I believe this is why Jesus said that the kingdom of heaven belongs to the children and that we must become like little children if we are to see it. A small child hasn't put on the armor yet. They are pure essence, without the trappings of ego and its respective emotional vice.

Building on this thought, the Enneagram vices we've been exploring can be seen as the seven deadly sins plus self-deception (type Three) and fear (type Six). Type One represents the deadly sin of anger. Type Two represents the deadly sin of pride. Type Four represents the deadly sin of envy. Type Five represents the deadly sin of avarice. Type Seven represents the deadly sin of gluttony.

Type Eight represents the deadly sin of lust. And type Nine represents the deadly sin of sloth.

As we unpack the stories and mine the broken places behind our "deadly sin," we can begin to do the work of creating space for new choices. And for lasting transformation to occur, one of those choices must include acknowledging that the emotional vice of our type is an addiction. It is an addiction born from the childhood assault on our inherent virtue. We must confront and surrender that addiction in order to open ourselves up completely to the journey from low to high awareness.

High awareness is embodied awareness. It is to no longer see the Enneagram as merely a two-dimensional drawing but to now perceive it as actually a three-dimensional sphere we step into, moving about freely and recovering our lost and broken pieces. First from wing to wing, then against and with our arrows, we begin to move where we need to, when we need to, learning to release the familiar—the addiction—in exchange for a truer, unencumbered lived experience. Until one day, perhaps, we find ourselves standing in the middle of the sphere—perceiving all of reality as it was meant to be witnessed, fully cognizant that we are all, in fact, connected. We are one with each other and creation itself. We all share the same DNA. Our commitment to growth, then, isn't just personal; it is a responsibility we have to one another.

So step inside. Because when you do your work, you help me with mine. When you heal, so do I.

Helping Others Heal

Our growth practices must also include strategies for seeing and supporting others with kindness and understanding—right where they are. It's a mistake for us to imagine that the way we perceive the world is the baseline for others as well or that others will want to be treated in exactly the same way we want to be treated.

224

One thing the Enneagram helps us to understand is how we can be more sensitive to the goals, desires, and pet peeves of all the other types and can make people's lives a bit easier by meeting them where they are. The following suggestions may help you with that.

For Ones

- Create space for their desire to improve things.
- Show them compassion for how self-critical they can be (remember that although they may seem to have impossible expectations for others, what they expect of themselves is even greater).
- Gently help them to see that there are often multiple paths to success and many good ways of doing things.

For Twos

- Create space for them to offer relational support.
- Show them genuine and specific affirmation for their gifts.
- Gently help them to connect to their own personal feelings and needs, which they may be sublimating in order to play the role of the Helper.
- Demonstrate your tangible affection for them when they aren't doing anything to help you or anyone else as a means of helping them to feel wanted and loved for who they are.

For Threes

- Create space for them to shine, demonstrating their strengths and other positive attributes.
- Gently help them identify ways to reflect more deeply on what true success means to them (beyond the surface level).

- Praise them for who they are instead of for what they accomplish.
- Encourage them to connect with their own emotions as a means of helping them to live their most successful life yet.

For Fours

- Create space for knowing and understanding their feelings without trying to minimize their pain.
- Affirm the value of their ideas and unique perspectives.
- Help them to identify what is working well in their lives, and gently encourage them to communicate positivity as a means of helping them to focus on what is good.

For Fives

- Create space for them to gather their thoughts, learn new things, and govern their own time.
- Express genuine interest in their intellectual knowledge and expertise.
- Help them identify ways to open up to diverse perspectives, especially ways of knowing that are body-centered or heart-centered.
- Encourage them to share more of their feelings with others as a means of helping them to be more present in their bodies and in important interpersonal relationships.

For Sixes

- Create space for them to talk through their concerns.
- Offer them reassurances as you help them identify ways to turn threats into opportunities, emphasizing how capable they have been in the past at dealing with challenges.

- Help them clarify their intentions behind problem-solving as a means toward helping them learn to envision the upside of all the possibilities the future holds.

For Sevens

- Create space for them to vocalize their ideas.
- Offer support for their natural inclination toward innovation and creating change.
- Gently help them identify strategies for handling negative situations, sadness, or pain.
- Encourage them to slowly begin to balance optimism with realism as they move toward a fuller spectrum of emotional experience.

For Eights

- Create space for them to take on demanding challenges that have significant impacts.
- Show them appreciation for their big-picture perspective and their concerns for issues of fairness and justice.
- Help them identify opportunities for expressing tenderness and connecting to their own vulnerability as a means of becoming truly strong and courageous.

For Nines

- Create space for them to support others and defuse emerging conflicts.
- Gently help them identify their own desires and perspectives and to unapologetically express them.
- Encourage them to act on their own behalf with confidence, without fear or hesitation, as a means of positively disrupting their inner and outer worlds.

Into the Unknown

> This is what transformation looks like: Deviation toward oneself.
>
> —Dr. Beau Lotto, neuroscientist

If you want to finally find and maintain emotional intelligence in your everyday life, pursue healing. You see, we are these emotionally wounded people being told to live more emotionally intelligent lives. But the latter can only come from healing the former. With self-acceptance, honesty, and kindness, we are invited to engage in practices that set us on the journey from vice to virtue—from low awareness to high awareness. We must recover the parts of ourselves that we've denied and surrender the masks we've been wearing to try to keep those places hidden. There are no life hacks when it comes to transformational growth.

As you do this work, I'd like you to take note of something that Polish American philosopher Alfred Korzybski once said: "The map is not the territory." I hope you now appreciate that the Enneagram can be a powerful tool for helping us traverse from the false self to the real self. But the Enneagram isn't you. The Enneagram is a map. It points us to the truth of who we are and who we aren't and lays out a path for our personal growth. But it's up to us to walk that path, face our shadows, do the work, and reconnect to our depths. Never confuse a model of reality with reality.

And the reality is, I can't tell you what you will find in the belly of the whale. I just know you need to go in. As Donald Rumsfeld once famously said, "There are known knowns. These are things we know that we know. There are known unknowns. That is to say, there are things that we know we don't know. But there are also unknown unknowns. There are things we don't know we don't know."

Doing this work means confronting our fears. It means laying down our defenses, the familiar, the comfortable. It means facing old wounds with honesty and self-friendship. It means walking a map with a vague sense of where we are going though not really sure of the altitude changes or steep ravines we might come across along the way—and being open to all of it. It means there are knowns, unknowns, and unknown unknowns. I don't know all you'll discover if you choose to walk the path. I don't know what shadows you'll have to face, what stories you'll need to confront, or what long-buried artifacts you might dig up on your expedition. But I do know that if you stay the course, you stand to discover the most precious unearthing of all: *you.*

NOTES

Introduction Something Isn't Right

1. Parker J. Palmer, *Let Your Life Speak: Listening for the Voice of Vocation* (San Francisco: Jossey-Bass, 2015), 16 (italics in original).

Chapter 1 The Enneagram at a Glance

1. Helen Palmer, *The Enneagram: Understanding Yourself and the Others in Your Life* (New York: HarperCollins, 1991), 10.

2. Sandra Maitri, *The Enneagram of Passions and Virtues* (New York: Penguin, 2005), 13.

3. Ian Morgan Cron, *The Story of You: An Enneagram Journey to Becoming Your True Self* (New York: HarperOne, 2021), 8.

4. Note that subtypes are not covered in this book. For a comprehensive exploration of all twenty-seven subtypes in the Enneagram, read Beatrice Chestnut, *The Complete Enneagram: 27 Paths to Greater Self-Knowledge* (Berkeley: She Writes Press, 2013).

Chapter 2 Emotional Intelligence

1. Travis Bradberry, "Why You Need Emotional Intelligence to Succeed," Inc .com, accessed October 5, 2022, https://www.inc.com/travis-bradberry/why-you -need-emotional-intelligence-to-succeed.html.

2. Purpose & Performance Group, "Unlocking EQ," accessed October 5, 2022, https://www.purposeandperformancegroup.com/unlocking-eq.

3. Tasha Eurich, "What Self-Awareness Really Is (and How to Cultivate It)," *Harvard Business Review*, January 4, 2018, https://hbr.org/2018/01/what-self -awareness-really-is-and-how-to-cultivate-it.

4. Corporate Leadership Council, "Driving Performance and Retention Through Employee Engagement," 2004, https://www.stcloudstate.edu/human resources/_files/documents/supv-brown-bag/employee-engagement.pdf.

5. Stuart Hearn, "Why Is Employee Engagement Important?," Clear Review, July 26, 2015, https://www.clearreview.com/how-does-employee-engagement-impact-performance.

6. Lisa Feldman Barrett, *How Emotions Are Made: The Secret Life of the Brain* (Boston: Mariner Books, 2017), 53.

7. For an in-depth explanation of these concepts, see Barrett, *How Emotions Are Made.*

8. Each of these five composite scales includes three subscales. I considered writing about all fifteen, but you would've had to take a sabbatical just to get through this book if I had.

9. Tasha Eurich, *Insight: The Surprising Truth about How Others See Us, How We See Ourselves, and Why the Answers Matter More Than We Think* (New York: Currency, 2017), 90.

Chapter 3 Self-Perception

1. Lee Glickstein, "Public Speaking and the Gaze of Attunement: Mother Mirroring and the Father Gaze," Speaking Circles International, February 13, 2011, https://speakingcirclesinternational.com/the-gaze-of-attunement/.

2. Carl Jung, *Modern Man in Search of a Soul* (1933; repr., Eastford, CT: Martino Fine Books, 2017), 111.

Chapter 4 Self-Expression

1. For more on this, see Lisa Feldman Barrett, *How Emotions Are Made: The Secret Life of the Brain* (Boston: Mariner Books, 2017), especially chap. 3.

Chapter 5 Interpersonal Relationships

1. Claudio Naranjo, *Ennea-Type Structures: Self-Analysis for the Seeker* (Nevada City, CA: Gateways/IDHHB, Inc., 1990), 38.

2. Peter O'Hanrahan, "The Enneagram Defense System: Access Points for Self Awareness and Growth," The Enneagram at Work, accessed August 9, 2022, https://theenneagramatwork.com/defense-systems.

3. Thomas Merton, *Love and Living*, ed. Naomi Burton Stone and Brother Patrick Hart (New York: Harcourt, 1979), 27.

Chapter 6 Decision-Making

1. Katie Moisse, "Hungry for Justice: Judges Less Likely to Grant Parole on Empty Stomach?," ABCNews, April 11, 2011, https://abcnews.go.com/Health/MindMoodNews/hungry-judges-grant-parole/story?id=13347415.

2. Gardiner Morse, "Decisions and Desire," *Harvard Business Review*, January 2006, https://hbr.org/2006/01/decisions-and-desire.

3. "Unpredicting with Stuart Firestein," *The Evolving Leader* (podcast), season 2, episode 1, January 20, 2021, https://evolvingleader.buzzsprout.com /1309339/7391524-unpredicting-with-stuart-firestein.

4. Robert A. Burton, *On Being Certain: Believing You Are Right Even When You're Not* (New York: St. Martin's Griffin, 2009), 103.

5. Beau Lotto, *Deviate: The Science of Seeing Differently* (New York: Hachette Books, 2017), 2.

6. Subtypes and instinctual sequences are part of more advanced Enneagram study and are not covered in this book.

7. Annie Murphy Paul, *The Extended Mind: The Power of Thinking outside the Brain* (Boston: Mariner Books, 2021), 29.

8. For more on this, see Carol S. Dweck, *Mindset: The New Psychology of Success* (New York: Ballantine Books, 2006).

Chapter 7 Stress Management

1. Annie Murphy Paul, *The Extended Mind: The Power of Thinking outside the Brain* (Boston: Mariner Books, 2021), 29.

2. Emma Seppälä and Kim Cameron, "Proof That Positive Work Cultures Are More Productive," *Harvard Business Review*, December 1, 2015, https://hbr.org /2015/12/proof-that-positive-work-cultures-are-more-productive.

3. Niraj Chokshi, "Americans Are among the Most Stressed People in the World," *New York Times*, April 25, 2019, https://www.nytimes.com/2019/04/25 /us/americans-stressful.html.

4. American Psychological Association, "One Year Later, a New Wave of Pandemic Health Concerns," March 11, 2021, https://www.apa.org/news/press /releases/stress/2021/one-year-pandemic-stress.

5. Paul, *Extended Mind*, 28.

Chapter 8 Face Your Fear

1. Don Richard Riso and Russ Hudson, *The Wisdom of the Enneagram: The Complete Guide to Psychological and Spiritual Growth for the Nine Personality Types* (New York: Bantam, 1999), 360–61.

Chapter 9 An Act of Courage

1. Peter O'Hanrahan, "The Enneagram Defense System: Access Points for Self Awareness and Growth," The Enneagram at Work, accessed August 9, 2022, https://theenneagramatwork.com/defense-systems.

2. James Hollis, *The Middle Passage: From Misery to Meaning in Midlife* (Toronto: Inner City Books, 1993), 116.

3. Dallas Willard, *The Divine Conspiracy: Rediscovering Our Hidden Life in God* (New York: HarperCollins, 1998), 11.

Chapter 10 Practices for the Path Forward

1. Beatrice Chestnut and Uranio Paes, "Gurdjieff, The Fourth Way, and the Enneagram for Inner Work: Self-Remembering," season 1, episode 46, *Enneagram*

2.0 Podcast, November 11, 2021, https://podcasts.apple.com/us/podcast/s1-ep46 -gurdjieff-the-fourth-way-and-the-enneagram/id1499745500?i=1000541519950.

2. For an in-depth discussion of the correlation between exercise and mental clarity, see Caroline Williams, *Move: How the New Science of Body Movement Can Set Your Mind Free* (New York: Hanover Square Press, 2022).

3. Kendra Cherry, "What Is Spiritual Bypassing?," VeryWellMind, December 6, 2020, https://www.verywellmind.com/what-is-spiritual-bypassing-5081640.

Scott Allender is an expert in global leadership and organizational development. Along with cohosting *The Evolving Leader* podcast, Scott regularly teaches Enneagram workshops and conducts typing interviews and emotional intelligence assessments for individuals and teams who seek to become more radically self-aware and cognizant of the impact they have on the world.